P9-EEJ-763

Pastoral Psychology

Pastoral Psychology

New Trends in Theory and Practice

Carlo A. Weber

Sheed and Ward, Inc., New York

Sheed and Ward, Inc., 1970

Library of Congress Catalog Card Number 73–101548

Standard Book Number 8362–1420–x

Manufactured in the United States of America

Contents

To
Karl Stern,
teacher and friend,
in partial payment

INTRODUCTION

Introduction

Language, C. S. Lewis wrote, can be a masquerade. "The percentage of mere syntax masquerading as meaning may vary from something like 100% in political writers, journalists, psychologists, and economists to something like 40% in the writers of children's stories. . . ." Syntax abounds in the field of pastoral psychology, most of it buried away in look-alike books. Some of these are little more than translations of psychological data for religious audiences; some are rather pretentious attempts at synthesis, effected by juxtaposing chapters of indifferent theology and poor psychology. Few are as meaningful as children's stories.

One should have good reason for inflicting another book on such a surfeited audience. I have no such compelling excuse, apart from the fact that this book does not pretend to an artificial synthesis nor, I hope, is it a mere translation. I am, to be sure, hopeful that some glimmer of a rapprochement between religion and psychology can be discerned in it. If it is there, it is because I am convinced that whenever a synthesis of religion and psychology does appear, it will be based upon their mutual discovery of the central position of the human person. I have tried to suggest that in the first chapter, "Psychology and Religion: The Two Solitudes."

In another place, I want to focus what little I know of theology and psychology on a problem critical to both: the phenomenon of human guilt. I also want to suggest that there are human experiences, e.g., a sadness explained as neurotic depression or spiritual desolation, which can change color and spots according to who's looking at them. It is only by wrestling with these problems that we may eventually establish some genuine communion between religion and psychology. Much of the present reconciliation between theologians and psychologists looks unfortunately like a shotgun wedding, with much strained and self-conscious "bending over backwards." I am not convinced that a blissful and sincere union is now, or even can be, cemented; but I am convinced that if it ever does happen, it will only be by clearing away our disciplinary preconceptions to take another look at the human experiences presented to both clinicians and pastors.

This book grew largely out of some summer workshops in pastoral counseling conducted at Loyola University in Los Angeles in 1966 and 1967. Not much lecturing was done at those workshops. The emphasis was placed squarely on experience rather than explanation. But ideas seemed to come out of them, and if it were not for the workshops, this book would not have been born.

For whatever value that birth may have, I am grateful to far more midwives than I can mention here. Fortunately for me, the midwives are also dear and close friends: Dr. Karl Stern of Montreal, Dr. Jim Gill of Harvard, Drs. Werner Mendel and Dave McWhirter of USC-Medical Center, Drs. Everett Shostrom and Richard Hinson of Los Angeles, Fathers Joe

Caldwell of Loyola and Norb Rigali of Cambridge and many others. The work of midwifery was also carried on most graciously by Peggy Mathison and Claudia Stadden, who typed the manuscript and served as hostesses, innkeepers and troubleshooters during the workshops.

To be sure, there are many, many more, who either appear anonymously in the pages of the book, or who have influenced the writing of it in other less manifest ways. They remain known only to me. But for their gift of themselves—a gift of incalculable beauty—I give these few words in return.

I also wish to thank the publishers for permission to reprint "The Field of Combat: Neurotic or Existential Guilt," which first appeared in the *Review for Religious,* Vol. 28, No. 2 (March, 1969), pp. 219–229.

All the quotations from the Bible are from the *New Testament,* edited by James A. Kleist, S.J., and Joseph L. Lilly, C.M. (Milwaukee: Bruce Publishing Co., 1956).

1. *Psychology and Religion: Two Solitudes*

For far too many years psychology and religion faced each other from out of the darkness of two solitudes, two worlds apart. More than anything else, a mutual suspicion marked the communication between them. For many theologians, psychology seemed basically a Jewish plot to undermine the Church. It was materialistic, deterministic and motivated by a calculated effort on the part of psychologists to usurp the traditional status of the high priest as confessor to the human race. Theologians were generally suspicious of phrases like Viktor Frankl's "medical ministry."[1] For many psychologists, on the other hand, religion was an archaic malaise, an opiate. Faith and the fear of hell were little more than devices to keep Christians subservient children. Religious experience was essentially a psychic phenomenon to be studied by phenomenological methods only. Psychologists viewed

behavior once thought to be manifestations of saintly mortification as really nothing but subtle forms of pathological masochism, and diagnosed martyrdom and other somewhat
unusual activities as simply expressions of hysterical conversion neuroses. The distance between the combatants in this
generally futile war could be portrayed by the difference in
their respective postures. It is a long way from being on one's
knees in the confessional to being on one's back on a couch.

Hopefully, this mutual defensiveness is gone, replaced today by many admirable efforts at effecting something of a
shaky, shotgun wedding between the former antagonists.
Such efforts are visible in workshops conducted to study the
relationship of psychology and religion, societies of religion
and mental health, etc., all of which have mushroomed in the
past ten to fifteen years. The newlyweds, however, show at
times a rather strained, self-conscious urge to cooperate, or
perhaps to conciliate, even at times to the point where ministers and psychologists seem bent upon switching their former roles; clergymen often sound quite a bit more like
counselors than ministers of the Word, and not a few psychologists deliver healing services that seem in fact to be
sacramental. Witness the burgeoning interest among psychologists in the phenomenology of the religious experience.
In this game of professional musical chairs, it is no longer a
simple matter to know who's sitting in what spot.

Similarities and Differences

The task of exploring similarities between psychology and
religion in such an historically antagonistic atmosphere is
precarious and possibly presumptuous. The differences between the two disciplines in theory, and between the confessional and the couch in practice, are more obvious than the
similarities. Theology, for example, is concerned with the
relationships of the self with God; psychology with the relationships of the self with others and with the self. These
objectives often appear to stand in conflict. Theology is nor-

mative and concerned with the region of the supernatural; psychology is inductive and concerned with nature alone. Theology is said to be concerned with the "heights" of human experience; psychology with the "depths." In this context, one author has spoken of psychoanalysis as an "inverted" religion.[2] The academic traditions out of which religion and psychology have risen are different. Psychology, at least in its clinical form, rose from a marriage of the medical tradition and the new science of the eighteenth century. It is concerned with observable phenomena, behavior and a description of that behavior. Theology is based on revelation. It is concerned with "believables" rather than "observables." And differences are apparent in practice as well. A listing of them serves to suggest some of the popular stereotypes that have contributed to the noncommunication of the past.

The God Within

It is obvious that some of these differences are more semantic than real. Freud and St. Thomas might have made strange bedfellows, but never so strange as their disciples, who tend to be more Freudian than Freud, or Thomistic than St. Thomas. Too often, the disciple manages to capture little of his master's complexity, and in his devotion, passes on but a shallow caricature of the great man's living insights. One difference, for example, between the two viewpoints allegedly lies in the fact that one studies the heights and the other the depths of human experience. Theology looks up and out. Psychology looks down and in. Is such a difference in direction real or semantic? What do these dimensions mean? To be up or down? To look upward or inward? Is it not possible that regardless of the presumed direction or vectors of our gaze, we might still be regarding the same object?

Religionists have long searched for the "God out and up there," the transcendent God.[3] But the Incarnation focuses our attention on the fact that God is not simply up and *out* there but *in* there, in creation, in our neighbor. If He is in there, in our neighbor who is a person, He is in that creature who is most "person" to me, in myself, in the most hidden inner core of myself which I scarcely ever encounter, but which may very well be what we have traditionally called "the image of God." We have historically paid lip service to the credo that "man was made in the image and likeness of God," but never really believed it. As the theologian now moves his gaze from the God "up and out there," to the God "inside persons," he becomes inevitably more personalistic and moves closer and closer to the viewpoint of the psychologist. And the psychologist, who realizes that fixing one's gaze intransigently and narcissistically inward becomes a closed process, must begin to look outward to transcendent experience to find the true self. Paradoxically, the theologian, in his pursuit of God, must ultimately look within to find the God who is without. The psychologist, in his pursuit of the self, must look without to find the self that is within. It is for this reason that many clerics and religious involved in sensitivity training geared towards group self-awareness comment that their experience was a very "religious" one. In what sense could it be called religious? There is no specific mention of God, no mention of transcendence. There is only the intense pursuit of the self within. This can only be a religious experience if the genuine pursuit of self can reveal the God who is somehow fused with the self. If so, the alleged differences in direction seem to be fictional constructs.

Another difference, which may be only semantic, is that psychology is a science and theology is not, depending upon one's definition of science. No matter how scientific psychologists would like to be, they are obliged to acknowledge that understanding people always leaves a mystery. In a counseling situation, especially, once you lose the mystery of the other person, you lose the other person.

There is, however, another difference between these two solitudes which is far more real. Communication between persons, we know, fails principally when the two communicants are not integrated, not put together, within themselves.

A distortion of communication follows when, for example, what one does is not what one says, and the dissonance or lack of harmony is apparent. It has been so with the communication between psychology and religion. The structure of man's understanding of man disintegrated somewhere in history. Psychology and religion both try to understand man, but both became disintegrated within themselves. The larger the rift within each of the disciplines, the wider the split between them. The long divorce between psychology and religion was a function of smaller disintegrations and divorces and splits within each. My objective here is to explore cursorily the common dilemma that historically split both psychology and religion within their own disciplines, and my hypothesis is simply this: when two disciplines are disintegrated within themselves, they will be disintegrated from one another. And, in fact, in both psychology and religion, taken separately, the view of man has been disintegrated. Restore the integrity of each discipline, and communication between them will follow.

Dualism in Theology

Psychology and religion have been disintegrated within themselves, I would submit, because of a common dilemma. In theology, it is called the Christological problem; in psychology, the body-mind problem. How do we explain the fusion, the coming together of spirit and matter, of mind and body, of the divine and the human? Psychology and religion have similar histories in their attempts to resolve these dichotomies. The principal *bête noir* in this historical drama is the radically dualistic solution of the dilemma. The tendency is to resolve the problem simply by a split between the two horns of the dilemma. It has historically been a temptation for theologians to resolve the problem of how to reconcile the presence of both divine and human natures in the person of Christ by simply denying one and affirming the other. Christ was simply human, because only the father was God, claimed

Arius, but he seemed divine. He was divine, answered the Monophysites and later the Docetists, and he only seemed to be human. It has been equally tempting for psychologists historically to resolve the body-mind problem in the same facile way. Man is but matter, wrote Hume; there is nothing else. He is but mind, answered the Idealists; the rest is illusion.

Dualism—a splitting of man into parts—left the theological view of man essentially disintegrated since the time of the early Christological heresies, and psychological view dismembered since Descartes.

Within ascetical theology, the long and venerable tradition of dualism reinforced the separation of the divine from the human, the soul from the body, the spiritual from the material. The Gnostics, against whom St. John inveighed, separated the children of light from the children of darkness, the elect from the uninitiated, and lost themselves in a megalomaniac, self-exalting identification with the mystic cosmogonies. They had employed the expression "Logos," or "Word," to describe themselves as the emanations of the divine idea. John, by using the selfsame description for Jesus in the introduction to his Gospel, was insisting, as emphatically as he could, that not among the Gnostic elite, but here, in the person of Jesus, the God-made-flesh, was one to find the true "Word." "In the beginning was the Word: the Word was with God . . ." (John 1:1).

Perhaps the clearest expression of the dualistic tradition is to be found in the philosophy of Manes and his followers, the Manichees. Here, two principles of creation, one of good and one of evil, create two quite different phenomena. The principle of good is the creator of the spirit; the evil genius is the creator of matter. Matter, therefore, is evil; and man imprisoned in matter must be to that extent, evil. It is imperative, from the context of such an ethic, to strip the self of the material in order to gain redemption. Sex is evil or of no account; involvement in material affairs is evil. Identification of woman, "mater," with material, primitive sources makes her at best suspicious. The humanity of Christ is a scandal. It is impossible to develop this theme adequately in the scope of this chapter, but suffice it to say that Manichaeanism generated a long tradition in the Church, remaining until the puritanical Victorian ethic of the last century.

The history of this inability to reconcile the divine with the human is exemplified in the separation of the two in St. Augustine's city of God and city of Babylon. Possibly as a function of his own personal life and his mistrust of the material forces within man, Augustine laid the grounds for the Jansenism which is still a part of Roman Catholic tradition. In the tenth century, the Albigensians, the Cathari, the Waldenses, the Beghards and the Beguines formed sects to practice the magic which would relieve man of his humanity. Perhaps the best way of suppressing one's humanity was the practice of communal masochism characteristic of the Fraticelli and the Flagellants of the thirteenth century so vividly depicted in Ingmar Bergman's film *The Seventh Seal.* The strange and ironic conclusion of this kind of repression of sexuality is that it inevitably led to some sort of genital excess. It is to this point that Aldous Huxley addressed himself in *The Devils of Loudun.*[4]

It is simple psychological fact that such repression always leads to another distorted expression. Energy repressed manages by psychic displacement to reexpress itself in some other form. Thus, the repression ethic of the medieval cultist generally produced a frenzied, uncontrolled, deterministic and orgiastic kind of ritual which, for reasons of rationalization and self-exoneration, were christened by some title of Christian religious ritual. The obvious sort of compensation that such repression must produce was found in the practice of the Black Mass, the witchcraft, the magic and the mysteries of the Luciferians of the thirteenth and fourteenth centuries.

From the time of the Protestant Reformation this dualistic tradition separated into two camps; and we have, as residual elements of those two traditions, a Protestant form, Puritanism, and a Roman Catholic form, which has been labeled Jansenism or neo-Manichaeanism. The Puritan ethic emphasizes that pleasure is evil and that one must mortify himself if he is to gain the good life. The utilitarian values of thrift, austerity and hyperresponsibility, are all vehicles for attaining that good life in a dichotomized situation. The Catholic variation on the same theme goes back to the time of the Belgian monk, Jansenius, who at Port Royal in the seventeenth century, under the influence of the Abbé St. Cyran and Mére Angelique of the celebrated family Arnauld, wrote a commentary on St. Augustine. The commentary emphasized man's dependence upon God's grace, his incapacity to perform good works of his own, and so gave a theological underpinning to the dualistic tradition. Through Irish monks studying in France at the time and through French Canadians, we are the inheritors of this Jansenistic tradition. It is not just by caricature that Catholics have been described as people for whom the only sin is a sin against the sixth commandment, and the only virtue is obedience. When the flesh is seen to be bad, passive responsiveness to the grace of God, so easily confused and identified with the simple exercise of authority, is the supreme value.

A sick, disintegrated theology of man leads inevitably to a sick spirituality. A man who is cut up into dualistic poles within himself can have only a cut-up asceticism. Nowhere was this disintegration more evident than in the life of the "Grey Eminence," Friar Joseph. The personal ambassador of Cardinal Richelieu to the courts of Europe during the seventeenth century, Joseph enjoyed a universal reputation for piety. His penitential practices, poverty, self-effacing humility and spirit of obedience were known to all. Somewhat ostentatiously, he was a familiar scene in his frayed and dirty grey soutane, head bowed, trudging on bare feet to represent France and Richelieu at the great conclave, where his poverty contrasted with the pomp usually displayed there. But it was this "holy man" who was almost single-handedly responsible for the continuation of the Thirty

Years' War in Germany and the slaughter of thousands of innocent lives, simply because it was in the political interest of the court of France that the war continue. How was it possible for this alleged man of God to perpetrate such an atrocity? The dilemma can be explained only in terms of a separation of the life of the spirit from the realm of human affairs. And we have these forms today. The Manichaean spirit remains. It lives in the asceticism that emphasizes the suppression of the flesh, detachment, the action of *agere contra,* the movement against one's self in order to be of value. It is involved in the sublimely ironic ethic that the good Christian is a God-fearing man, rather than a God-loving man. In Puritanism, of course, we have the same ethic in a rather different tradition. But in both, there is an emphasis on practiced humility and docility as the supreme virtues and the suppression of the individual in favor of the community. To this end, we have developed the most exquisitely effective ways of enabling the individual to disappear by elevating the importance of religious habit, of common life and of the virtues of obedience, humility and docility exclusively.

The problem is that fear of the material leads inevitably to a kind of fascination. We become quickly preoccupied with what we fear, and with the preoccupation, a fascination results. The fear of one's self leads to a fascination with one's self, a narcissistic self-preoccupation. It is a psychological commonplace that fear is a poor motive. If we repeat to a child over and over again that he should not touch the radiator because, if he does, he will be burnt, it is almost certain that he will ultimately touch the radiator. We cannot avoid danger just by trying to avoid danger. We simply become preoccupied with it.

From this dualism arose a secularistic, even at times a kind of schizophrenic piety. Christians tended to separate the love of God from the love of man, and in doing so, pressed on heroically toward union with God while ignoring the fate of their fellowman. The hypocrisy of the "righteous" man who attended Church regularly, contributed to Church-sponsored organizations and fund-raising drives but had no time for others on a personal level made a charade of religious worship. This modern pharisee in the temple was most graphically depicted by Ingmar Bergman, whose films over and over again stressed the theme that righteousness kills innocence just as surely as passion does.

C.S. Lewis remarks in one marvelous passage that we have spent much time trying to press man on to a divine love past simply human love when the real job is to get him that far.[5] These are disintegrated forms of spirituality, separating the spiritual from the material. Basically, we do this with the Incarnation. Do we really believe, for example, that there was a God-man? How many people would be appalled if they heard a sermon directed to the humanity of Christ which admitted that Jesus did, after all, get his feet dirty, had occasional bowel movements and laughed and wept and tired and loved and hated? For Christians, Christ is not a man; we have been obliged to make Him a superman. We cannot really accept the humanity of Christ because we do not accept our own humanity and can only invent an inhuman spirituality. If these, then, have been the traditional ways of presenting God to man, is it any wonder that one hears the cry that God is dead? The irony, of course, is that Christ's message and His person have been so obscured historically that young people must turn away from Christianity to find precisely what Christ was talking about.

Dualism in Psychology

Curiously enough, the same dualistic dilemma, the same problem and solutions, are found throughout the history of modern psychology. The psychologist's basic dilemma is the classic body-mind problem. He must always be concerned with the relationship of the body to the mind, of matter to spirit, of dust to dreams, of the mysterious and fascinating inner action of the psychosomatic relationship. How is it possible that emotional and intrapsychic conditions can produce physiological symptoms? How is it possible for the body to speak for the psyche? That it does is simply a scientific fact. But how this interaction takes place is a puzzle which science has not yet resolved.

The first solution to the dilemma in modern psychology was Descartes' "ghost in the machine." There were, he said, two entities, a spirit and a body, interacting through the pineal gland. The two were as distinct as the ideas we have of them; the explanation of their interaction a simplistic bit of magic. Faced with such a dualistic dichotomy, psychologists were obliged to choose sides in an either-or tug of war. The history of psychology from Descartes until the psychosomatic theories of Goldstein, Meyer and others was predominately a description of the war between the Idealists in Germany and the Empiricists or Materialists in Great Britain. In attempting to resolve the Cartesian split, each had fallen into a system of reductive monism, with one side claiming that everything was really matter and that spirit was merely a delusion, while the other insisted that everything was really spirit and that matter was merely an illusion. The war was waged until the latter part of the nineteenth century when the psycho-biological schools became ascendant. Descartes' original dualism has been rejected; body and mind are simply seen as two distinct operating functions of one psychosomatic unit. This by no means resolves the thorny questions of the mode in which this interactive monism functions, but it does indicate the trend away from the original Cartesian dualism.

Through time, in both psychology and theology, the problem of polarities has been solved in the same way. In psychology, the body-mind antinomies have been resolved in terms of the psychosomatic theory emphasizing both the effect of the psyche on the body and the body on the psyche. This psychosomatic view of man could be said, by way of a theological analogy, to be an incarnational view of the person. In theology, too, the antimony between the divine and the human, the spiritual and the material, and the tradition of dualism which separated the two, has given way to an incarnational monism. The force of the Second Vatican Council has been precisely to reemphasize the central place in Christian history of the dogma of the Incarnation. However it happened, God did become man, and in that fact the dualism of the divine and the human is inescapably destroyed. Christ himself becomes the personified fusion of the polarities. And the fact is vastly more important than an explanation.

Disappearing along with the dualities is the kindred dualistic asceticism, now replaced by an incarnational one. This view basically presumes that if the divine and the human were fused, there must be something gracious about humanity, about the material, that would tolerate such a union. Dualistic asceticisms that picture one's union with the divine via the suppression of the human must give way to an incarnational asceticism which describes the union with God through the perfection of the human.

I do not intend here any disquisition on the ramifications and implications of these twin traditions in psychology and religion. Suffice it to note that the dualistic dilemmas in both disciplines have resolved themselves historically in the same way. And the common solutions point to a fusion *focalized radically in the importance, the value, the significance and the uniqueness of the human person.* Our current revolution is founded on that common solution. The revolution in psychology is against a hyperscientific compartmentalized view of man; the revolution in theology is against dualistic asceticisms which degrade the human. With the humpty-dumpty man created by scientific psychology and a dualistic theology put back together again, the two disciplines may communicate to one another with some harmony rather than the former dissonance.

Psychological Maturity and Sanctity

Psychology and theology have suffered from a common problem, the tendency to separate; and they have come to a common goal: the wholeness of the person and the search for *oneness,* with God, with the self and with the other. The goals of both disciplines have a shared ground in terms of self-discovery, the discovery of what it means *to be,* to be mature, to be able to love.

In psychological terms, this goal is expressed through several characteristics. First, we seek the independence of the person, the comfort in one's uniqueness, one's selfness. After all, the purpose of growth—biological, psychological and spiritual—is separation. The prime analogue for all growth is the separation of the fetus from the uterus. The fetus in the mother's uterus is biologically a parasite. It must be expelled. If it is not expelled, the life of both parent and child is threatened. The process of growth from that point on is a gradual process of weaning, of leaving, of separation. This is sometimes a very difficult thing for parents, teachers, counselors and superiors to accept. But however difficult it may be, it is certainly ontologically true that a parent's job is done only when the child is able to leave; that a teacher's job is done when the young student can rise and say "I disagree with you," providing, of course, he has good reasons for doing so; and a counselor's job is done when the counselee can say "I no longer need you." A superior's job is done when the individual can exercise his religious vocation and his calling with initiative, integrity and self-reliance. All of us are witness to the tragedy of the "possessive mom" and to the tragedy of the surrogate mothers—teachers, counselors and religious superiors. It is amazing the degree to which most psychopathology in religious life is immediately related to the presence of some "possessive mom."

But independence and self-acceptance must be counterbalanced by a realization of the fact that one is, after all, a *needer,* that one is separated and does need others. To do this there must be growth out of one's primary narcissism, out of the feeling that the world is there simply to serve me. In all of this, there is a balance of dependence and independence, a poised equilibrium between the dependence of the satellizing child and the independence of the autonomous person.

The same balance is characteristic of the spiritually developed person. Before God, man can see himself as nothing. Indeed, in many respects, before God, I *am* nothing. But this fact can be and has been exaggerated in our ascetical tradition and leads to prevailing feelings of worthlessness and chronic sinfulness. The spiritual analogue of the underlying feelings of one's worthlessness, so characteristic of all neurotic attitudes, is the feeling that one is essentially sinful. It is true that before God I am nothing and that before God I am totally dependent. But that is not the whole truth because my value before God is also extraordinary. This aspect also can and has been exaggerated historically. The Pelagian heresy suggests that man does not need God's help in order to gain perfect sanctity. But the balance of the truly spiritual man lies somewhere between the feelings of worthlessness and sinfulness on the one hand and the feelings of spiritual omnipotence on the other.

I find no place where this balance, expressive of both psychological maturity and of sanctity, is better expressed than in one section of the *New Testament*. Mary, aware of the announcement of the angel that she is carrying within herself the body of the Messiah, goes to her cousin Elizabeth and announces this fact to her. In the announcement she utters the magnificent prayer we call the *Magnificat*. There one finds her awareness of this awesome presence and the awareness also of her personal unworthiness, of her nothingness. She says to Elizabeth, "My soul reflects the glory of God ... because He has seen the *lowliness* of His handmaid."[6] In this statement one finds the recognition of her sense of dependence. But the essential thing is that she does not stop there. The next lines carry these words: "But He that is mighty has done great things in me."[7] And this, in turn, is a recognition of the fact of her worth before God.

Too long have we spiritually struck our breasts and repeated over and over again the phrase "Lord, I am not worthy." It is true, but it is not the whole truth. With Mary, we must, if we are to attain the twin goals of both psychological and ascetical maturity, be able also to say: "He that is mighty has done great things in me."[8]

Notes

1. Viktor Frankl, *The Doctor and the Soul* (New York: Alfred A. Knopf, Inc., 1957), pp. 261-280.
2. Karl Stern, *The Third Revolution* (New York: Doubleday & Co., Inc., 1954).
3. John Robinson, *Honest to God* (Philadelphia: The Westminster Press, 1963).
4. Aldous Huxley, *The Devils of Loudun,* 1st ed. (New York: Harper & Row, 1952).
5. C.S. Lewis, *The Case for Christianity* (The Macmillan Co., 1943).
6. Luke 1:46-49.
7. *Ibid.*
8. *Ibid.*

THEORY

THEORY

2. The Field of Combat: Neurotic or Existential Guilt

There is no domain in which the acute problem of communication between theology and psychology is more evident than in the experience of guilt. Stormy encounters on the nature and origins of the experience, its place in human development and its effects on human lives continue without much hope of resolution, largely because the language, the symbols and the context of the discussion are not the same for all the contestants. The field of combat is common to all, but the rules of the game are not the same. A split-level mode of communication has prevailed.

The experience of guilt, then, is the common playing field for theologians, psychologists and lawyers. But for each it means whatever the methodological conditioning of his own discipline obliges it to mean. For the moral theologian, it has generally suggested reprehensibility, culpability, blameworthiness, sin. For the lawyer, it means, specifically, responsibility before the law, civil or ecclesiastical, or criminality as determined by legal canons. And for the psychologist, in sharp contrast, it implies rather a first-level symptom, the crippling expression of a depreciating self-concept, perhaps the residue of a superego-oriented childhood training.

When the discussants in the dialogue use the same word to denote such utterly different things, communication soon dissolves into futile bickering over semantics. Guilt is sin; guilt is crime; guilt is symptom. The vocal sounds one hears in the dialogue alert the same signals; but the phenomena signalized are not the same. In such a conversation of nonmeanings, a fruitless and frustrating collision is inevitable. It is like approaching a railroad crossing without the slightest assurance whether the waving semaphore symbolizes an approaching train or an unimpeded right-of-way. One would be better off without the semaphore in such a case; and so we might be better off without the word "guilt." In many instances, the "guilt-language," as the "God-language" or the "soul-language," or other similar efforts at noncommunication might best be scrapped, that we might attempt an uncluttered look at the phenomenological realities, and then allow a new language to emerge to fit the reality. Orwell's "New-speak," or Cattell's[2] crypto-scientific system of operational definitions in psychometrics may, however wild they first seem, be something of the answer. We might well avoid the confusion that always arises from previous connotations of a word by introducing entirely different sound associations.

The present state of affairs, then, is largely one in which the language of guilt tends to divide authorities rather than to aid communication between them. When the psychologist hears his legal associate describe a man's guilt in court and watches him step nimbly through what appears to be a maze of legal fictions, he finds the process frightfully objective, abstract, impersonal, inhuman. But the lawyer is not really describing the psychologist's "guilt." The theologian is properly horrified, on the other hand, when he hears the psychologist's attempts to gloss over the reality of guilt and his description of guilt as some neurotic myth. This, to him, is a form of "psychologizing"—foggy, anarchic and sentimental. But the psychologist is not, in fact, describing the theologian's "guilt" either. Indeed, if he is loyal to his methodology, he has nothing to say of it. One could, of course, continue with this litany of misunderstanding. The cross-cultural impasses are often as evident as the semantic circus of an international diplomatic conference.

Definitions of Guilt

Though it may be next to impossible to draw meaning from this semantic labyrinth, we are, nonetheless, stuck with it. It's a value to note that within the verbal entente orientations which have traditionally set the contestants apart do emerge. It may be helpful to try to clarify them. For the psychologist, guilt is strictly a subjective phenomenon, a feeling that can become almost the pervasive element of one's inner experience. The psychologist is little concerned about the external, objective counterpart of the experience. His world, as a clinician, is the perceptual world, not precisely the accuracy of the precepts. Whether one's feeling of guilt, therefore, is rooted in antisocial actions or in an interiorized, guilt-ridden self-concept is not precisely the point. It is now the individual's feeling, and the psychologist deals with it as such. He also realizes that the intensity of the experience is not necessarily in proportion to the quality of an external action or event. One individual may experience crushing guilt subsequent to running a red light at a deserted intersection; another may remain blandly guilt-free after bludgeoning a harmless old lady's skull. Such a feeling of guilt is clearly not the function of some specific external action. But it is the correlate and the expression of his own inner awareness of his value, or rather the lack of it. The inner awareness is the point of differentiation for the psychologist.

For both the moral theologian and the lawyer, however, there is an objective emphasis in the philosophy of guilt. An objective norm which has been violated is the criterion according to which one assesses guilt. That norm, of course, is not the same for both. For the lawyer, it is the civil or common law. For the moralist, it is the "will of God," expressed either through Canon Law, or the magisterium of a teaching Church, or the sacred books or the natural law. But in each case, the norm is an external one; and guilt is the function of a violation of that norm. Once that has been established, the legalist can turn his attention to the degree of individual culpability, e.g., knowledge of the existence of the norm, consciousness at the moment of violation, presence or absence of overwhelming emotional or physical duress, etc.

So long as we can reasonably assume some subject-object dichotomy, these two arrangements appear to be quite different. The moral theologian and the lawyer, both with their own specific articulation of the norm of behavior, regard guilt as the individual's posture before the law. The psychologist sees it more as the individual's posture before himself. That there is room for overlapping of these dimensions is as true as the fact that the subject-object dichotomy is not crystal clear. But, with that qualification, the criteria are different, and so also are the semantic worlds built around the two points of view.

Unfortunately, the tradition of morality in the West has been heavily legal since the days when the Latin rite was imposed on the Western Church. And with the Latin rite came the Roman tradition of law and legal prescriptions. The language and the emphasis of the Western Church when addressing itself to questions of morality and guilt has been on the side of law. Moral textbooks became classic examples of legal casuistry. Room was always left, to be sure, for the "subjective," as preserved in the distinction between formal and material sin; but the bulk of any discussion inevitably turned about a consideration of the objective, or material guilt. Scarcely more than a condescending nod was given to the presence of the subjective element as the final determinant of sinfulness, with something of a begrudging acknowledgement that that aspect, after all, was the most important. But no effort was expended until very recent times in attempting to provide some phenomenological map of the subjective. Perhaps the futility of that prospect obliged the moralists to turn their attention to the legal puzzle that was, after all, more intellectually satisfying and a good deal more comfortable. One would suggest, mindful of the discussions swirling about Pope Paul's Encyclical *Humanae Vitae,* that it is clear that the legal emphasis is still the prevailing attitude of the official Church. The rupture within the Church is precisely a function of the person vs. law approaches to morality and guilt.

When the law becomes the criterion for human behavior, the stage is set for casuistic thinking about morality. This implies a mental "set" in which one is concerned chiefly with the degree of deviation from the norm. How far, for example, can I deviate from the statement of the law and still be safe? Or, at what point of deviation do I stray from the area of safety to the domain in which I must be classified as a sinner, if it be a moral law, or a criminal, if it be a civil law? Legal guilt is the consequence of straying outside the latitude which the law allows. In that area the legalist-moralist conducts his conceptual jousting. Only recently have attempts been made to bring about a marriage of the law and the personal in the various modes of situational ethics. And this, of course, is both the effect of the communion of psychologists and theologians and a stimulating reinforcement for it. The norm becomes more an ideal which one strives to approach continuously throughout his life rather than a law from which one deviates.

Neurotic Guilt

The genesis of neurotic guilt, as described by the psychopathologist, follows a commonly described nuclear process most brilliantly outlined originally by Karen Horney. There are four discernible stages. The process begins with a faulty personality development in childhood. The child, whose first self-concept, as such, is the result of the interiorization of the value placed upon him by his parents, sees himself as those significant people in his life see him. If the child is rejected, unwanted, ignored, neglected, he begins at an early stage in psychological development to see himself as unworthy and unlovable. This is a fairly obvious situation and need not be explored at any length. The rejected child anticipates rejection from others because that is the extent of his experience; and he can, in gross instances, unconsciously provoke rejection by hostile, abrasive conduct, precisely because of this expected response pattern. Such a child is almost bound to "always hurt the one he loves." At the other extreme of parental reaction, the child can be overprotected in his early years. The result is the absence of any process of growth into independence. The custodial love of the parent prevents the possibility of growth, and the child remains weak, helpless, dependent. In terms of the growth of a self-concept, the child will tend to see himself in the same manner and behave as such. No one is unfamiliar with the suffocating, devouring, destructive mother-child relationship, described first by Strecker, who coined the phrases "Mom" and "Momism" in his classic, *Their Mother's Sons.*[3] The notion has become virtually a household word since, and it is even more popular with the expression of theories of a burgeoning matriarchal society.

Interestingly enough, the effect on the self-concept of the child of both rejection and overprotection is approximately the same. These are simply two sides of the same coin. In either case, the child is not being valued for himself. The rejected child is not loved at all; the overprotected child is not loved, except as the mirror-reflection of the mother whose narcissistic needs are projected on him. In both instances, the child disappears. This is also true, but not to the same extent, in the situation where the parents' love for the child is conditional. The child is loved providing he follows certain ground rules established by the parents. Ground rules are essential, of course, but they ought not to be the condition for acceptance. If they are, the child sees himself as valuable and lovable only as long as he continues to fulfill the regulations for being loved. He must continue to perform the tasks prescribed; and, in time, the task-oriented process becomes a way of life. Whether the child is rejected, overprotected or conditionally loved, the effect, in varying degrees, is the same. The child perceives himself as inadequate, unlovable, helpless or constantly in need of proving his value.

The moral analogue to the psychological feeling of ineptness or inadequacy is the feeling of guilt. The latter is merely a translation of the same feeling from psychological language to moral language. To say, in a psychological context, that I am weak, flaccid, incompetent, unlovable is the same as saying, in a moral context, I am bad, sinful, guilty. The difference here between the neurotic guilt and genuine forms of responsible guilt lies in the difference between the phrase "I *am* bad" and the statement "I *do* bad things." The former is a description of the basic personality of the self-depreciating neurotic; the latter a description of occasional activity. The most apt expression of the neurotic guilt feeling was given me, quite incidentally, by a woman patient who was incredibly scrupulous. For her, every action was a sin. In a therapy session she remarked, rather in passing, "You know, sin is in my veins." And with this cryptic observation, she sums it all up. "Sin, badness, is as much a part of me as my very blood. It describes my life, my being, my essence, as it were. And since I am, in essence, sinful, every action, which, in fact, is an expression of my nature, must be sinful. I shall either discover it there, as the scrupulous person does, or I shall do those very things which will confirm my view of myself in the eyes of others." This, indeed, is the epitome of neurotic guilt.

The same statement in other words was made by another patient, a 25-year-old woman in perpetual need of proving to herself her sexual acceptability. Leaving the office on one occasion, she turned and announced, "You know, you don't really like me. You like me only because you have to." There is, of course, no response to this. What she is really saying is that she is convinced that she is unlovable and that any signs I might show her to the contrary are merely a function of my professional posture. It has to be that way for her to preserve the long-standing image of herself as essentially unlovable, evidence to the contrary notwithstanding. The same essential neurotic guilt was continually expressed in another young patient's fear that she would do harm to the students in her Grade III class. She avoided touching them and washed her hands repeatedly for fear that somehow, if she made physical contact, the badness in herself would be communicated to the children, and she would harm them in some way. In all these instances, the same kernel is present: the prevailing feeling of one's own worthlessness and unlovableness which, transposed into a moral context, is equivalent to one's sinfulness.

Neurotic guilt, when deeply rooted in individual experience, becomes a way of life. The tortured person literally swims in a sea of guilt; he lives and breathes it in a world shot through with badness. Behavior patterns are then learned largely as a way of sustaining the self-as-excrement vision. There follows a curious inversion of values. Virtues become the means for sustaining that vision; vices are the foes of the vision. A "virtue" that supports the neurotic vision, for example, is the deference-to-the-point-of-obsequiousness which is a way of coping with guilt. Or, the guilt-ridden person might launch into bursts of frantic industry in order to compensate for badness and unworthiness by work. The hope remains that the work alone will be seen and a mask will be placed by that means over one's intrinsic badness. The virtues sustaining the neurotic vision are often commonly rewarded forms of behavior: industriousness, thrift, social approval, etc. The lace-curtain Irish brand of deception, within which milieu one insists that "dirty laundry" must be kept home, or that one should strive ever to keep the best foot forward resembles such "virtue." At all costs "appearance" must be preserved so that the danger that one will be seen for what he really is, or rather for what he perceives himself to be, must be avoided. The virtues of the Protestant ethic are not unlike these.

In even more destructive forms, the guilt-ridden person can make a virtue of his own self-destructiveness by thinking of it as a martyrdom. He becomes in his own view an heroic "victim" soul, impaled to the cross with his Savior, signalling to the world about him that there is no suffering quite like his. His self-inflicted martyrdom, which becomes in time more of a martyrdom for everyone else around him than for himself, becomes the final self-immolating virtue in a sequence of contrived behavior designed by the unconscious specifically for the purpose of preserving the neurotic vision. This is not to say that one need not suffer in a world tainted with tragedy. For if one is truly free to love, one must also be free to hate. There can be no human freedom without both joy and tragedy. Freedom of choice necessitates the freedom of being able to choose pain rather than pleasure, hate rather than love, suffering rather than joy. But this is the pain and agony that is the corollary to freedom. It is in-built in nature. It is, however, one thing to accept that inescapable fact and martyrdom as a possible condition of personal life. It is another to choose a fancied martyrdom as a means of preserving one's view of oneself and the world.

"Vice," on the other hand, describes whatever action threatens to undermine the established and defensive behavior pattern. Laziness, procrastination, indulgence in fantasy and failure to observe social canons are wrong because they endanger the barricade that one has erected between himself and society, a barricade that is necessary because of the fear that if society sees him as he really is or thinks himself to be the reaction will be disgust. The tragedy of such a value system is simply that it is not the supposed vices, but rather the supposed virtues that are rotten.

We unfortunately baptized this twisted way of life in the

past by a Christian education that emphasized sin and guilt. Jansenism was condemned by the Church, to be sure, but Christian educators and administrators seem not to have been aware of that condemnation. Until recently, we educated our children into a world of fear and guilt. We assumed in practice a Jansenistic theology which sees man as essentially corrupted by original sin. Religion, therefore, like the lace-curtain Irish social ethic, became a means of warding off moral disaster. We became obsessed with the danger of temptations, the horror of self-realization, the value of self-inflicted martyrdom, preoccupation with sin and a conviction that we will be overrun by our passions if they are not repressed or denied. Formalized religious training became a series of prohibitions and negations, a catalogue of "don'ts." And in this religious context the sense of guilt was firmly reinforced.

The irony of the situation is simply that fear as a motive does not effectively assist us in avoiding the supposed danger. Indeed, fear, as was pointed out earlier, is but a step away from fascination. The fear of falling from a high place can lead to a momentary desire to jump. The fear of small pain can lead to a need to inflict small pain on oneself. Overwhelming fear leads to overwhelming preoccupation and a self-destructive fascination with the very object of fear. The fear of sin and guilt, taken exclusively, leads rather toward sin than away from it, as Oraison argued so effectively in *Love or Constraint.*[4] The lesson ought to be clear; we cannot avoid sin simply by trying to avoid sin. The agony of the psychotherapist in confronting such forms of neurotic guilt is that it frees its hold on the suffering person only very reluctantly. When the sense of guilt becomes so deeply imbedded in the individual's total world of experience, the system relinquishes it as begrudgingly as though it were its own life. Such a deeply entrenched attitude establishes a resistance to change as relentless as the body's own biological immunity system.

Since it is the suffering person's whole, historical world of experience that has been both parent and home for the sense of guilt, no amount of rationalization, analysis, support or discussion can supplant it with another mode of perception. The only thing that can replace a long and cumulative experience of the self and the world is another experience. And all systems are working precisely to ward off such an experience. The process is slow, frustrating, capricious. It demands all the resources, personal and technical, that the therapist can muster.

Ontological Guilt

It would be grossly simplistic to suggest that all experience of guilt is neurotic and prebehavioral. Guilt awareness can follow either an honest admission of one's destructive behavior or an existential sense of the tragic in life. Not to admit this possibility is to embark on a course that would strip man of his freedom and responsibility. It is frightfully dehumanizing to rationalize away responsibility by reducing all guilt-experience to mere "neurotic feelings" for which we are unaccountable. When we do so, we offer only an insipid palliative to replace a genuine anguish felt before the human situation. We must acknowledge that we are at our best capable of actions that can destroy our relationships with ourselves, others and God. This mode of destruction is real, not neurotic. And we cannot whisk that capacity away by a form of psychologizing that can only demean humanity.

The doctrine of Original Sin, as I understand it, is essentially a ratification of the awareness of the capacity for both light and darkness in our lives. The darkness is partly of our own making and partly a condition of our existence. But there can be no light without darkness, wakefulness without sleep, sun without shadows, love without hate. Our life is necessarily framed by both joy and tragedy. To dispel the darkness, the tragedy, the existential possibility for genuine guilt is to rob man of his vitality and leave a bland, bloodless shell in his place, a man who cannot love because he cannot hate, cannot unite because he is too afraid of disuniting and cannot love and serve God because he cannot sin. The theologian must be concerned with these ultimate values; he cannot stop with the psychologist's description of neurotic guilt. He must concern himself with the capacity for ontological guilt. Theological guilt, therefore, arises from the free actions of man rather than from the neurotic misconception of one's depraved being. And it is rooted in the knowledge that there is no freedom to love without freedom to hurt.

Associated with such a capacity for real ontological guilt is the existential awareness of one's own contingency, of the presence of the seeds of nonbeing somewhere at the core of being. Life bears within it the shadow of death. There is no "Eros" without "Thanatos"; the seeds of life are strewn with the seeds of death and nothingness. Consciousness of this capacity for nonbeing is the *Urangst* experience of Kierkegaard's *Sickness Unto Death*,[5] the original experience of the continental existentialists from Schopenhauer and Scheler to Sartre and Camus. This awareness awaits for no specific action. Death, or the threat of death, is simply ever there. And with it there is another experience of guilt neither consequent upon destructive actions placed and acknowledged nor flowing from a neurotic self-depreciation. Consciousness of nonbeing is existential guilt. It is primitive anxiety, a dread that awaits a cause. No one with vital sensitivity can escape it. The existential psychiatry of postwar Germany, of Binswanger and Buydendijk and Boss, bred in concentration camps, crying with the forlorn residue of two world wars, obliged to stare at life with often hollow eyes, to draw meaning, as Frankl did, from living with death, plaintively recalls the psychic death experience. American psychologists imported war-born existentialism to the United States, injected it with the peculiar brand of American optimism, cut out its heart and left it a bland, insipid *weltanschaung*. We have not learned that we cannot have mountains without valleys.

Existential Guilt

The existential guilt-experience is mystery. It is the testimony to the inexplicable intermingling of good and evil, joy and suffering, glory and tragedy. To rob life of its mystery is to steal its soul. It must be there in the meeting with life. It must be there in the meeting with life as it is lived most fully, in persons, in the world of "Thous." To take away the mystery of life, the mystery of the other person, is to lose life, to lose the other person. We meet with anguish as well as joy. We do not meet unless we can separate. We cannot live unless we can die. What we can only haltingly describe is utterly essential to the existential guilt-experience.

Of the three faces of guilt, neurotic, theological and existential, there are common properties and common symptoms. The sense of anguish is not different; the expression of fear and dread is not clearly different. They can only be distinguished on a deep dynamic level. It is no good to play God here and presume to label experience with one of these three categorical tags without deep and exhaustive understanding of the life-experience and style of the individual who feels the guilt. There are many ways in which the experiences seem the same, but there are also some common indices to distinguish neurotic guilt from the other two. Neurotic guilt is observably disproportionate. One feels guilty for the slightest of offenses because of one's need to feel guilty. Neurotic guilt cannot be appeased. The psyche feeds on it with an insatiable hunger and journeys on an endless search for its food. There is no "absolution" for neurotic guilt. The scrupulous person, as all confessors know, is the most chronic recidivist. And neurotic guilt carries with it an unmistakable narcissistic flavor. It is a twisted cry for attention. One who cannot tolerate the exquisite agony of standing for himself must find devious ways of inviting a response from others. The plaint of the neurotically guilty individual is a bent seduction, a withered eye that gleams with a siren's beckoning. But there is no love.

In the experience of ontological guilt, be it theological or existential, there is always the capacity to hurt, offend and violate because there is the capacity to love. Christian confession is thus not intended to salve the conscience of the neurotic. It is rather a public statement that the penitent has simply not loved God enough. The neurotic guilt experience precedes the awareness of any conscious act by which one's lack of love is manifest. Ontological guilt is the awareness of a conscious act or state of being that succeeds conscious loving and living. The purpose of confession is to absolve the experience of ontological guilt; the purpose of therapy is to absolve the experience of neurotic guilt. In that sense, psychotherapy precedes confession. Its purpose is to assist the suffering person in his efforts to arrive at the point where he is truly free to sin and to experience real guilt. The neurotic is free neither to love or to sin. The therapist stands by, present to the experience of the patient, as he struggles through the labyrinth of his guilt feelings to emerge into freedom. Only then can he experience theological or existential guilt; only then is he free to be truly guilty. Freedom brings with it that tragic sense; and it is the abiding sense of freedom and tragedy, of love and guilt, of beauty and ugliness that unites the saint and the sinner.

Notes

1. George Orwell, *1984*, 1st American ed. (New York: Harcourt, Brace & World, Inc., 1949).
2. *Cf.* R. B. Cattell, *Handbook, Children's Personality Questionnaire* (Champaign, Ill.: Institute of Personality and Ability Testing,1959).
3. Edward Strecker, *Their Mothers' Sons* (Philadelphia: J.B. Lippincott Co., 1946).
4. Marc Oraison, *Love or Constraint* (New York: P. J. Kenedy & Sons, 1959).
5. Soren Kierkegaard, *The Sickness Unto Death* (New York: Doubleday & Co., Inc., 1954), pp. 141-278.

3. *Mental Illness: Disease or Myth?*

"Their madness is not true madness. Our sanity is not true sanity."[1] With such provocative language Ronald Laing, the controversial British psychiatrist, delivers his crippling blows at the foundations of the scientific and pseudoscientific legerdemain that has for generations enjoyed credibility under the title, "Abnormal Psychology" or "Psychopathology." Since the Greek Hippocrates, and more recently the German Kraepelin, a mass of scientific literature has developed, delineating with some finality what it means to be mentally ill and how such illness is to be discerned and treated. But for the past dozen years, it has become rather popular to question whether this mountain of literature is science or myth. Abnormal psychology is now a study in transition. In a frighteningly genuine sense, the psychopathologist does not know what he is talking about. No one knows with any certainty what it is to be abnormal, pathological or ill in a psychological sense. What one does know is behavior.

"We can see other people's behavior, but not their experience," writes Ronald Laing in *The Politics of Experience*.[2] Beyond behavior one can make only inferences about the sanity or insanity, sickness or health, adjustment or maladjustment, comfort or pain involved in that behavior. That experience is private.

As is so often the case, the determination rests on a decision about criteria. According to what standard do we judge other people to be sick or well, adjusted or maladjusted, diseased or healthy? And upon that criteria, the validity of scientific literature falls or stands.

Medical, Psychometric and Social Criteria

Historically, there have been three basic models for judging mental illness. They are not mutually exclusive, of course, but they are a convenient means for grouping many different criteria together. One is medical; the second is psychometric; and the third is social.

The Medical Model

According to the medical model, mental illness is best understood by means of an analogy with physical illness. In organic pathology one assumes that there is somewhere in the interacting organic systems a diseased organ which manifests itself in external signs which we call symptoms. By carefully observing these symptoms, a pathologist renders a careful and scientific diagnosis, on the basis of which he recommends therapy and hopes for some manner of cure. The model is essentially a fairly simple one, and its appropriateness when dealing with physical disease is quite apparent. If there is a diseased kidney or a malfunctioning adrenal cortex, this aberration shows itself to the patient and to his physician in discernible patterns which can be read according to the catalogues available in any good lexicon of medical pathology. Through years of research therapeutic means have been developed to eliminate the diseased organ or rectify the malfunctioning system. And the treatment subsequently effects a cure if the symptoms have been diagnosed correctly.

Because psychopathology was born out of a medical tradition, this model has been translated into the area of alleged psychological illness, so that psychopathology became the study of diseased organisms, also manifest in symptoms which could be diagnosed and cured. But locking oneself within a conceptual system tends to prevent one from asking essential questions about whether or not the system is applicable at all. And psychopathology is one of those unique sciences which can ask questions it cannot answer. Where, for example, is the diseased organ in the case of mental illness? Is it in the mind, the body, the soul or the psyche? And what, after all, are they? What is sick? What is malformed? What symptoms are we diagnosing and according to what criteria? Or, finally, what can one possibly mean by a "cure"!

For years the medical model remained unquestioned. It enjoyed a venerable tradition. In the fourth century before Christ, the father of medicine, Hippocrates, began to clarify the symptoms he observed under carefully designed Greek rubrics. He was the first to speak of "post-partum psychosis," phobias, delirium and hysteria. The word "hysteria," from the Greek, *hysteros,* was chosen to suggest "a wandering uterus," a disease characteristic of women and one with clear neurotic overtones. All these symptoms, according to Hippocrates, had an organic basis. The diseased organ was generally located somewhere in the brain, the organ of thought, and the malfunctioning could be explained by the presence of bile, phlegm, body fluids or bad humors somewhere in the endocrine system.

The assumption that psychic manifestations had a physiological root and, therefore, could be understood according to some physiological model prevailed, with some deviations, through the period of medical awakening until about the third century A.D. Psychic disturbances were generally thought to depend upon the quality and operation of brain tissue. On the basis of these qualities Galen, the father of modern anatomy, described nine basic temperaments, a conceptual fable still employed by purveyors of amateur psychology. Nonetheless, Galen personified the apex of Greek and Roman scientific efforts to understand human behavior.

With the decline of Rome and through the Dark Ages the scientific approach gave way to a theological one in which psychopathology became demonology. The disease was not due to the presence of some alien chemical substance in the blood stream, but to the presence of the devil in the possessed person. Sickness was identified with sinfulness. Symptoms, however, remained the same: markedly bizarre behavior patterns which could be easily observed. A diagnosis was still rendered, and therapy still administered in some form of exorcism. In the fourth century Marcellus described a disease he called "lycanthropy," the name chosen to describe the behavior of a wolf-man, a "werewolf" or a "steppenwolf," who wandered at night, howled like a wolf and allegedly had been transformed into one by the devil. The therapy recommended for the disease was a "laying on of hands." The high point of the tradition of demonology was reached with the publication of the text *Malleus Maleficarum* by two Dominican monks in 1484.[3] It described in detail the behavior of witches and other possessed individuals and the manner in which they were to be pursued and handled by punitive measures. In its own way, it was as complete a compendium as any text of medical pathology.

This new science of unearthing witches became the principal agenda for the inquisition, a pastime which provided curious entertainment through most of the Middle Ages. Out of this came a very formalized system of demonology not unlike the medical model. Mental disease was excluded from the area of medicine and put into the class of systematized superstition, which included not only possession by the devil but also by other natural forces endowed with a new animism and with magical powers. The sylvani and fauni, the larvae, incubi and succubi were all carefully classified. The lunar cycle was also held accountable. Crazy people were held to be under the influence of the moon and labeled, as a consequence, "luna-tics." The psychiatry of Hippocrates and Galen had become, via superstitious animism, a study of the ways of the devil and of lunar forces. The cures for such possession included religious exorcism, self-flagellation and such curious frenzies as the St. Vitus Dance, a collective convulsive agitation that was originally hoped to cure the disease called "Tarantism." In Southern Italy, this disease was thought to result from the bite of a tarantula, and to be cured by a body-wrenching dance to music which came to be known as the "Tarantella." In the seventeenth century, however, an anonymous physician exposed himself to the bite of the tarantula and discovered that there was no effect. And gradually, apart from some residual local customs that remained in the United States until this century, the St. Vitus Dance disappeared, though the Tarantella remained.

The medical-scientific tradition regained strength primarily during the enlightenment of the sixteenth century. Paracelsus recognized that "abnormal" behavior was not the result of possession, but of a disease, the cause of which was some natural phenomenon. In the newly regained medical tradition, it was Henry VIII who was responsible for the foundation of one of the first mental hospitals. In 1547 he founded St. Mary's of Bethlehem. But conditions at St. Mary's were less than therapeutic. Visits to the patients were made about once a year, in April usually, by the attending physician who prescribed "bleeding" to cure the individual of his disease. As testimony to this mode of "treatment," the name Bethlehem became corrupted to "bedlam," a word still used to describe such conditions. The deplorable state of mental hospitals was rectified to some degree through the work of Phillipe Pinel in 1793 in France. When he became physician-in-chief of the Hospital Bicetre, Pinel discovered vast pandemonium and he begged the Commune to release fifty patients from their chains. This was done on September 2, 1793. His treatise on insanity and the statistical work of his successor, Jean Etienne Esquirol, introduced a measure of humane hospital treatment for those conceived to be mentally ill. It would be, however, a gross overstatement to suggest that Pinel's work has been continued to the degree that conditions in mental hospitals are no longer wretched. But that is not our point.

The medical model received its greatest impetus from Emil Kraepelin, who died in 1926 after systematizing, as no one previously had done, all the classifications of mental illness according to careful diagnostic categories. With a strong semantic orientation, he studied a vast number of cases. By the age of 28 he had published his volume *Psychiatric, Ein Lehrbuch,* 2,500 pages of painstakingly careful diagnosis.[4] It was he who coined such phrases as "dementia praecox," or "precocious madness," a term since abandoned in favor of the word "schizophrenia." Dementia, according to Kraepelin, was the result of biochemical imbalance, particularly affecting the sex glands. He also coined the phrase "manic-depressive psychosis," and others, many still in vogue.

The assumption that there was some physiological basis for psychopathological behavior received its greatest reinforcement in the early part of the twentieth century when it was discovered that general paresis, originally thought to be psychogenic, was really the function of latent syphilis. It was optimistically hoped that if paresis was found to have a physical basis, it would be only time before science would uncover the physical causes for all other psychopathological manifestations.

From the time of Kraepelin until contemporary psychiatry, the medical model has prevailed, leaving a legacy of terms not unknown to the average reader of any psychiatric literature. Schizophrenia, paranoia, the distinction between neurosis and psychosis, etc., are all part of the language of the medical tradition. The advantages of such a vocabulary are evident. It provides us with simple, scientifically clear, communicable ways of understanding behavior that seems to be at odds with what most of us commonly do. The diagnosis of such diseases provides us with a point for orienting a therapeutic process. The basic assumption that psychopathology was analogous to physical pathology, with an identifiable and curable organic base, remained relatively unchallenged until recently.

The Psychometric Model

The scientific preoccupation is also revealed in the second of the great traditions, the psychometric one. Pinel and his successor, Esquirol, had first used a statistical method of determining the range of illness among the patients in their hospitals. The statistics used, of course, were crude in the sense that the analysis was based on a mere counting and classification of different forms of behavior. But the advent of scientific psychology, principally in central Germany in the Leipzig laboratory of Wilhelm Wundt, and the discovery by Weber and Fechner simultaneously of a psycho-physical scale of measurement, encouraged statistical models. Spurred by the work of Galton and then Pearson in England, these methods became increasingly prevalent. Individuals were considered mentally ill, not on the basis of some discernible organic pathology, but on deviation from some determined normal standard. Human behavior was ranged along a normal curve. Anyone familiar with the overworked bell-shaped curve and the laws of chance, knows that the normal range is 68.3 per cent of the total population, encompassed within one standard deviation to the right or the left of the mean. Whatever human behavior could be counted within that range was considered normal. Whatever patterns of behavior were rare enough to be included in the upper or lower three to five per cent would be considered abnormal. And a new criterion was established. Instead of one borrowed from medical science, the new criterion was one of normalcy or abnormalcy according to statistical distribution. And psychopathology inherited a new set of terms. One spoke now of deviants and abnormals, rather than psychotics and neurotics.

The medical model had enjoyed a presumed authenticity on the basis of the assumption that psychopathology could be as exact as medical pathology. The psychometric model enjoyed similar authenticity on the grounds that we could measure variations of behavior on a psychophysical scale with an exactness roughly equivalent to the physical sciences. The medical model had gained impetus when it was discovered that paresis was actually the result of syphilis; and the psychometric model gained impetus when it was discovered by Weber and Fechner that human reaction times could be measured with precision on a physical scale. It was consequently hoped that all psychological behavior could be some day spread along a physical scale. Proponents of each model could easily argue that success in one instance implied that similar success awaited further research in all instances. To date, it has not been proven true.

The Social Model

While the medical model was based on scientific medicine, and the psychometric model on developments in the physical sciences, the third great model, a social one, was based on studies in the social sciences. Instead of speaking of health or disease, or normal or abnormal, the social scientists spoke of being adjusted or maladjusted. The first norm was physical; the second was statistical; the third was social. The mental hygiene movement in the United States, spurred by the work of Clifford Beers and Dorothea Dix, emphasized the belief that mental health is a function of one's adjustment to society. Social conformity became the norm of mental health, just as average behavior and the absence of disease, or homeostasis, had formerly reigned as virtually unquestioned criteria. Once again there was a different vocabulary. Instead of speaking in medical terms of psychosis and neurosis, or in statistical terms of deviation one spoke in terms of "reactions." The label of schizophrenia was supplanted by the phrase, a "schizophrenic *reaction*," depression by "depressive *reaction*," obsession by "obsessive-compulsive *reactions*." The very word "reaction" suggests that the criterion of health was to be understood not in terms of one's intrapsychic activity but in terms of one's response to a social environment.

However, as Ronald Laing trenchantly remarks, "What is it to be socially adjusted to an insane society?" Emily Dickinson's poems often expressed this dilemma:

> Much madness is divinest sense to a discerning eye;
> Much sense the starkest madness.
> Tis the majority in this, as all, prevails.
> Assent, and you are sane;
> Demur, and you're straightway dangerous and handled with
>   a chain.[5]

For better or worse, these three criteria have colored our previous understanding of psychopathology. But at this point in the history of the understanding of variations of human behavior, all three are seriously challenged. Thomas Szasz, in 1956, wrote an article and then a book, *The Myth of Mental Illness,*[6] in which he suggested with strong emphasis that it was impossible to understand psychological phenomenon according to any model, that there was neither a diseased entity nor symptoms. Talk of diagnosis and a cure, therefore, was simply mythical. On the other hand, the inability of the psychometric model to distinguish the quality of deviation rendered it ineffectual. On the basis of deviation alone, one could not distinguish the genius from the moron, the creative artist from the psychopath, etc. And the mental hygiene or social model left no room for a valid investigation or change in a society which itself may be partially diseased.

In contemporary discussions a new criterion has emerged, one which stands in almost direct contrast to the mental hygiene model. Instead of the bland, colorless, "adjusted" individual, contemporary therapists are thinking in terms rather of "creative maladjustment" as the ultimate objective of therapy and growth. It is no longer enough that one live without crippling disease, or within a broad range of people who can be classified as statistically normal, or in accommodation to a society that itself reels with the crippling malaise of hypocrisy and irrelevance. The ability to perceive the fitness of the society in which one lives and to stand creatively, though not petulantly, alongside it is now more frequently considered to be characteristic of the "healthy" person. With this criterion, man's perception of himself comes full cycle, for no one fulfills this criterion more effectively than the prophet of the Old Testament. In language as appropriate to pre-Christian as to contemporary society, therapists are announcing that the healthy person in our society today is the prophetic person.

The "View from Within"

To the three classic models or traditions which have dominated the field of psychopathology many others have been added to further confuse an already hybrid study. The most consistent thread running throughout these neo-criteria is the "view from within." Locked within the medical, psychometric or social model, scientists and/or therapists must see the patient from outside, and apply to him designations or labels from outside. All the newer approaches tend to stress the importance of trying to understand the person from *within* his experience rather than to label it from without. It is, of course, impossible to identify perfectly with the experience of the so-called neurotic or psychotic person. "I cannot experience your experience. You cannot experience my experience. We are both invisible men. All men are invisible to one another. Experience is man's invisibility to man."[7] Experience is essentially subjective. We can know another's experience only vicariously in terms of analogies with our own. But the fascinating quest is that we should try to reach across the chasm that separates us to identify more closely with the other's experience, futile though that prospect may ultimately be. It is the quest of that shared experience that is the hallmark of the new psychopathologies. In this respect, they approach mental illness from an entirely different point of view. From the history of literature, of autobiographical anecdotes written by individuals who themselves have suffered some manner of psychotic breakdown and from thousands of case histories, a new and mighty body of literature is fast growing. Self revelations of the experience of mental illness often give us information that calls much of the previously accepted data-from-without into serious question.

In one way or another, we are stating, as many literary figures have said, that it is vastly more important to try to get inside the skin of the other person than to plaster designations on him from a social, medical or psychometric world outside. Kaplan,[8] Levitas,[9] Arieti,[10] Laing[11] and many others regard psychopathology from this stance. To illustrate the difference, let us juxtapose the autobiographical statements of several persons hospitalized or treated at one time or another for "mental illness" with the psychiatric nosology under which they were diagnosed and treated.

Depression

More scientifically, depression has been described as: . . . an affective feeling-tone of sadness, probably the commonest type of complaint in psychiatric patients. Depression may vary from a mild downheartedness or feeling of indifference to a despair beyond hope. In the milder depressive syndrome, the patient is quiet, restrained, inhibited, unhappy, pessimistic and self-depreciative and he has a feeling of lassitude, inadequacy, discouragement and hopelessness. He is unable to make decisions and experiences difficulty with customarily easy mental activities. He is overconcerned with personal problems. Some depressed persons are petulant, querulous and distrustful. In somewhat deeper depression there is a constant unpleasant tension. Every experience is accompanied by mental pain and the patient is impenetrably absorbed with a few topics of a melancholy nature. Conversation may be painfully difficult. He is dejected and hopeless in attitude and manner. The patient's dispirited affective attitude is projected toward his environment which reflects his dolesome outlook. He feels rejected and unloved. He may be so preoccupied with depressive ruminations that attention, concentration and memory are impaired.[12]

Let us turn now to a patient trying from the very depths of depression to describe what he felt. This was difficult for him to do for he was markedly slowed down in speech and movements (a behavior characteristic of some depressive states known as retardation). He spoke in a sad, plaintive, at times tearful and sing-song tone of voice, which was sometimes so low that it was hard to hear him. There were many long pauses between sentences, and what is written took many times longer for the patient to speak that it does to read it. Here, as recorded, is what he said:

Everything seems to be contradictory. I don't seem to know what else to tell you, but that I am tearful and sad—and no kick out of Christmas. And I used to get such a boot out of it. . . . It's an awful feeling . . . I don't get a bit of a kick out of anything. Everything seems to get so sort of full of despair . . . I can't get interested in other people. I only seem to be interested in my own self. Can you offer me any advice in any way? . . .

Sometimes you seem to have a load of friends and yet nobody you really love . . . You feel awful lonesome . . . You just feel low . . . not a laugh nor a kick out of anything . . . It's all so sort of vague and hollow—nothing behind it . . . I hear and see everybody who comes to work so full of smiles and laughter and happiness. With me, it's not like that at all. And why is it that every once in a while I feel it's all going to end in disaster?

I feel so sort of what I call "empty"—nothing in back of you like when you're feeling yourself . . . You go to bed and you dread each day when you feel low like that . . . And I try to keep saying to myself, like you say, that I haven't been that bad that I should have to punish myself. Yet my thinking doesn't get cheerful. When it doesn't get cheerful, it makes you wonder will it all end in suicide sometime. . . .

I don't seem to have much feeling to want to go places—to concerts like I used to and back to work. There just doesn't seem to be anything perking. Do you think I've improved at all? . . .

I don't know why I don't get some help from praying. I ask God to help me through. I suppose it's my trial—guess I deserted the Lord for a long time. . . .When you feel low like this it all seems so hopeless. You dread the holiday and the long weekend. . . .This low feeling is so horrible. . . .

I cried terribly when the family left Sunday. If only I could be like they are—healthy, be one of them. The old fight seems to be gone . . . I can't seem to say that I'm going to get well with any real conviction. It all seems so shallow.[13]

Schizophrenia

Again, schizophrenic reactions are generally said to be recognizable through odd and bizarre behavior apparent in aloofness, suspiciousness, or periods of impulsive destructiveness and immature and exaggerated emotionality, often ambivalently directed and considered inappropriate by the observer. The interpersonal perceptions are distorted in the more serious states by delusional and hallucinatory material. In the most disorganized forms of schizophrenic living, withdrawal into a fantasy life takes place and is associated with serious disorder of thought and profound habit deteriorations in which the usual social customs and personal care are disregarded.

It is generally considered that the schizophrenic is incapable of effectively harmonizing his drives and inhibitions through mature adaptations and defenses. He has failed to develop a satisfying concept of his body and a clear or stable self-concept. He is often unclear in his goals, or his aspirations are so demanding or inflexible that they exceed his talents, persistence and drive to mastery. Thus he is deficient in his capacity to assess clearly the realities of the world. Interactions with others are characterized by immature processes of communication, thought and adaptation.

In psychoanalytic terms, the schizophrenics represent those who have failed, due to either somatic or psychogenic forces, to evolve the ego integrative processes or strengths necessary to resolve flexibly conflicts between their (id) drives and overdemanding superego attitudes and aspirations. They are thus defective in the capacity to adapt to the social demands confronting them and to their own drives, and thereby they lack a harmonious self-concept and ego ideal with clear goals and motivations. Much of their adaptation is made, instead, through partially satisfying regressive or fixated infantile behavior.[14]

But here is the personal account of a so-called schizophrenic:

Because I am I, an odd piece of egotism who could not make the riffle of living according to the precepts and standards society demands of itself, I find myself locked up with others of my kind in a "hospital" for the insane. There is nothing wrong with me—except I was born at least two thousand years too late. Ladies of Amazonian proportions and berserker propensities have passed quite out of vogue and have no place in this too damned civilized world.

Had I been born in the age and time when the world dealt in a straightforward manner with misfits as could not meet the requirements of living, I would not have been much of a problem to my contemporaries. They would have said that I was "possessed of the devil" and promptly stoned me to death— or else disposed of me in some other equally effective manner.

But because the poor, deluded taxpayers of America insist on the delusion they are civilized, they strain themselves to the breaking point to keep institutions for our care in operation. Then when they break down under the strain of trying to live up to the standards they set for themselves, the officials, whom they have appointed for the office, pronounce them insane—and they are committed to institutions.

I know I cannot think straight—but the conclusions I arrive at are very convincing to me, and I still think the whole system is a regular Hades itself. But there is nothing I can do about it—for I have been relieved of the responsibility of trying. It is just another of the vicious cycles that are forever whirling

about our destinies. And it is just my hard luck it whirled me
into an insane asylum. Here I sit, even though I was one time
a so-called intelligent member of society. I doubt that my
vision had ever great depth or wide scope even though I did
make a conscientious effort to live up to the demands of civili-
zation. I must have had a fair share of intelligence, or I could
not have conducted myself according to the rules as long as
I did. But now I cannot conduct myself as the rules set forth
because something has broken loose within me and I am insane—and differ from these others to the extent that I still
have sense enough to know it—which is a mark of spectacular
intelligence—so they tell me.[15]

The sample suggests the degree to which the actual lived
experience suffers in psychiatric translation.

The foundations of this new approach rest heavily upon
phenomenological and existential philosophies born in postwar central Europe, and introduced to the United States by
May,[16] Maslow,[17] Rogers,[18] many analysts and others. Emphasis is upon self-development, individual maturity, development and growth. One speaks more of being
"put-together," of the integrity of the person's organismic
systems and his self-realization, rather than of his ability to
function, to adjust, to live within a normal range or to con-
form.

In the remaining sections of this chapter, we shall try to
illustrate the two basic ways of viewing mental illness—ex-
perientially from within and diagnostically from without. The
core experience around which abnormal, deviant, maladjusted or individually experienced behavior turns is what
could be called the personal response to stress. Stress as it has
variously been defined by Selye[19] and others, is the compos-
ite of those conditions in the environment—social, organic or
physical—to which we must learn in some way to adjust.
Selye describes stress as an aggregate of physiological reactions in the organism, operationally defined as "that collec-
tion or syndrome of physiological reactions which one always
perceives under stressful conditions." In this sense, stress is

the observable physical reaction in the organism, not the external causes of those reactions. We are here speaking of stress, or stressors, as the factors that produce those physiological reactions rather than as the observable physiological reactions themselves. These agents are commonly described under three convenient titles: frustration, conflict and pressure.

Frustration

Frustration, essentially the thwarting or impeding of some drive, assumes first of all that there is some motivation, a drive or movement toward a goal or object. The movement may serve to reduce tension and maintain homeostasis, in the classic deficiency motivations of which Maslow speaks,[20] or it may be self-discovery, self-actualization, goal-seeking or growth motivation. Motivation and drives are never unimpeded in our society, nor should they be. Many things can block either tension-reduction or growth, and so the sources of frustration are virtually limitless. One can be frustrated because of the loss of a love-object, the death of a lover, or generalized social obstacles to one's growth. Or one can be frustrated because of some deficiency in the area of specific goal-orientation: the incapacity to achieve what one wants to achieve, as the awkwardness of the clumsy boy, coupled with his desire to show finesse on the athletic field, or the groping struggle to find the right words to express a personal experience. There are also the direct obstacles in one's environment: rules of society, speed bumps, bureaucratic red tape, etc. All of these frustrations involve the blocking of some drive.

There are in this analysis two assumptions. First, there can be no frustraton where there is no motivation. The autistic child or the apathetic individual is not frustrated because there is no drive toward either socialization or exploration. Secondly, wherever there is a drive, it will, in our society, encounter some frustration. The only alternative to the encounter with frustration is regression to infancy for the fear of it, a back-to-the-womb abdication from the human struggle. Self-acceptance, therefore, requires acceptance of the human situation as well.

Conflicts

Closely allied to the correlation of frustration and motivation is the concept of conflict. No man is truly simply motivated. In a world of complex goals, there must necessarily be conflict between varying motives. The classic approach to these conflicts is Lewin's double-approach, double-avoidance, and approach-avoidance classifications.[21] For Freud, too, the conflict between id and ego and super-ego was the essence of neurosis and of conflict. The pleasure principle versus the reality principle or libidinal needs versus societal demands constitutes the crucible of conflict and neurosis.

Such a conflict was clearly illustrated in the following letters I received from a young man torn by the conflict between his personal drives, as he understood them, and the demands of society.

> "November 15
> ... things have not been well at all with me personally. I went into a state of complete mental and physical discolor and have been under the constant care of a physician. I guess I'm just weak but find myself unable to face the fact of being alone, and miss my homosexual contact and relationship which puts me in a state of depression due to lonesomeness and lack of physical release. I'm fighting harder every day to hold on, but think sometimes it will overcome me. . . .
> My physician knows the situation and has me under medication for mental depression and physical exhaustion. I almost gave up several weeks ago, but find myself struggling thru again. If only someone could understand what a homosexual goes through, fighting life, Church and reality. There are times when there seems no way out or escape. It's either do and be happy, or don't and suffer. . . . I will not go to——— as I do not feel there is anyone there to understand. I've been

told to do too many different things to solve my situation, and it won't work—such as marriage, etc. . . .

November 20

I want to be with————, and yet I know it's no good, because I just become involved, but he does compensate for lonesomeness and satisfies the desires which exist. This is where I become pulled between Church and life. I cannot accept one for the other. I know my seeing this man is wrong, but on the other hand, it fills my need for companionship and satisfies my desires as well as filling a vacancy that only human flesh can fill, and by this I mean the presents of human life. . . . I do fear the future due to the fact that I am a homosexual and I have found that there is no solution of getting around it. . . . Before I found the Catholic faith I had no fear of the hereafter, but I'm so convinced that it's wrong in the sight of Almighty God, and yet He provided me with this life to lead and to tolerate. What did He mean for me to do? Why did He put in me such a state of life? Why does He wish to torment me and punish me to live a life like this? No matter where you go, where you live, the curse still follows. Father, you say you will understand, and I know you do, from a knowledge viewpoint, but you'll never experience the heartache and desire for something that is offending God, rotten in the public eye and a complete disgrace to humanity, but yet God makes man in His own image. How can this be? Every day is a complete struggle because you have to fight against temptation constantly and this is no picnic. You feel that you are doomed and cannot face public opinion.

Often the conflict can exist on various layers or levels of the personality. Apart from some advocates of the behavior-modification school, there are few therapists who believe that it is appropriate to deal with conflict on the symptomatic level only. Often enough the conflict can be itself a symptom constructed to mask a deeper conflict. The medical report of a young nurse who was for a short while a patient is illustrative.

Yvette was 22 years of age, slight of build, dark brunette,

wide-eyed, alert and quite attractive. She was admitted to the hospital after a suicide attempt in which she shot herself through the chest with a pistol. Brief elements of the patient's history were gathered in the pretesting interview to supplement the data from the psychiatric interview. The patient was the next to the youngest of six siblings. The family appeared to be characterized by emotional outbreaks. The father, a cold, distant, authoritarian and unapproachable person, was also a sometime alcoholic. The patient's feelings towards him, as indeed the rest of the family's, ranged from toleration to outright hatred.

Yvette remembered that as a girl she was a "tomboy" who loved sports, hunting, swimming, etc., and was not as a rule too popular with other girls. She noted also that her brothers seemed to her to be rather effeminate. She attended convent and Normal schools, sustaining very high grades throughout. Her first menstruation was late, at fifteen years. At the time, she was not bothered by this—indeed appeared to have no desire for the onset of womanhood. Her sex instruction was minimal, none from the family or school, and inaccurate information from other girls. As a young girl, she was repelled by sex.

Yvette left for nursing school feeling that her home town was too dull and that she would like the opportunity to travel occasionally. Throughout nursing training, she felt that she was disliked by the other student nurses because she tended to be flirtatious with doctors and patients in an attempt to gain their attention. She had met her present boyfriend several years before. He was married and seeking a divorce which his wife would not grant. The patient had been intimate with this man for several years and had had one abortion. She felt no guilt about the relationship and claimed it was her first experience, a genuine love. Sexually she took the active part in sex play and admitted that in this relationship, she wanted to please and hurt the man. To inspire his jealousy, she had a brief affair with a young doctor "to get even" with John after an argument and separation. The suicide attempt followed another argument with him. Despondent, she contemplated an overdose, but John took the pills out of her purse. Perhaps he suspected that such an attempt was possible. She had threatened suicide several times before. The night of the suicide attempt she was drinking heavily and she shot herself early in the morning. Then she called her girl friend who passed it off lightly. She was finally found by the girl friend and another boy. She claimed to have suffered no pain and was never unconscious.

The symptomatic conflict in Yvette's situation was the pull between her love for a married man and the moral code which prevented her from having him. The inability to resolve this conflict led to a very serious suicide attempt. But in therapy she discovered something else. Historically, she had always fallen in love with men whom she could not have —other married men, doctors in the hospital where she served as a nurse, a hospital chaplain. Inevitably, each was for her unavailable. In her love for these men, another conflict appeared: the need to love and be loved versus the fear of a loving commitment and what it would demand of her. In loving an unavailable man, she could feel her needs satisfied and still not be threatened by the actual demands of a living love relationship. Thus the overt symptom-conflict was unconsciously constructed to mask the deeper unconscious conflict that she could not tolerate. In therapy it is interesting to note that the symptom-conflict constructed about the love for the married man dissolved when the underlying conflict was revealed and dealt with. Therapy was therefore dedicated to the resolution of a deeper fear. If the therapist, however, had directed his attention to the resolution of only the symptom-conflict, by way of saying, "Either marry the man or give him up," there would have been no resolution, and the underlying conflict would only have created further conflicts in the future.

Pressure

The third stress agent or stressor is pressure. Pressures neither block motivation directly, nor do they produce conflicts.
I prefer to think of them as drive-exponentials, the exponent
or intensity of a drive raised to a power. If, for example, one's
ambition to succeed in college is intensified by parental demands for success plus the kind of competitive pressure
placed by the schools, and if in this way the drive is raised
to successive powers, the pressure simply becomes overwhelming. One sees this in the failure of the overachiever. It
is a commonplace that the curve of learning correlates posi-
tively with motivation to a certain point, and then, after a
leveling off, a negative correlation ensues between excessive
motivation and learning or performance. This decrease of
learning ability results from the stress of too much pressure.
In the face of any stress, everyone has his particular breaking
point. That point at which the stress becomes so excessive
that the individual cannot continue his normal functioning is
the point at which we can consider a pathological reaction
of some kind.

Life Space

There is another way to consider the stress relationship with
the environment. Anthropological studies in the area of territoriality suggest another concept.[22] Each animal species
enjoys its own territory, its own space. One researcher found
specific measurable and concentric spheres in the life space
of distinct animal species.[23] For each, there were unalterable
distances marked by different sets of responses. When the
animal in question perceived an alien species preparing to
penetrate any of the three spheres, his reactions changed
markedly. At first, within the first sphere which Heidiger
called the "critical zone," the animal tended to stand and
watch the alien carefully, warily. If that zone were crossed

and the alien approached even more closely into what Heidiger called the "flight zone," the animal turned and fled. And if, finally, the alien managed to get even closer, into a "fight zone," there came a point when the threatened animal inevitably stopped, turned and fought back. What was remarkable in this otherwise commonplace phenomenon was that each of the zones remained measurably constant for any distinct animal species.

Every member of the human species has his own life space, too. For each, there is a point when penetration by someone who is perceived to be a stranger into the subject's psychological space produces a wary watching, a cautious reserve to be maintained until the approaching alien is identified more adequately. If the stranger is seen to be inimical in any way, there are subsequent flight and fight reactions as the zones of the psychic space are progressively penetrated. The zones, unlike the animal species, are surely different in distance for each individual. Experiments in what constitutes the comfortable distance that separates or unites different people, the ease or difficulty with which different individuals tend to touch one another and the sensitivity of feeling physically close or far apart are all modes of determining the life space zones for varying persons. But whatever the differences, the zones are surely there, and they must be respected.

Sensitivity to the zones of the personal life space can also be an accurate barometer for the progress of rapport between therapist and client. Moving closer and further away as the client's mood alters and as the relationship progresses is an incalculably effective way of assessing the closeness and the variations in the emotional relationship between the two. It may very well be the function of the therapist to penetrate the client's zones gradually and sensitively, moving at the pace and willingness of the patient, until the flight and fight zones are eventually reached. The duration of this process depends heavily on the dimensions of the client's critical zone, but with time, one must pass the phase of hesitant examination, move through the seas of fear and contact the need to fight. When the client can finally express his anger, he may only then become convinced that what he perceived to be an alien species was not alien at all.

Defenses Against Stress

Whatever the source of stress, every individual constructs his own special defense against it, a defense system which reflects his general life-style. He may, after the manner already suggested in the "territoriality" analogy, use either a "flight" or "fight" response characteristically. Or he may employ a "task-oriented" or "defense-oriented" mode of response, finding refuge from stress either in ever more frenetic busy work or in a constellation of unconscious defense mechanisms, rationalizations, reaction-formations, projections, intellectualizations, and so on. But the style of defense is not really the significant criterion in determining what may be pathological. All of us use defenses that are consistent with our normal pattern of behavior—some attack, some withdraw, some intellectualize and some somatize. Honest self-analysis readily reveals our particular style of coping with stress. What distinguishes the pathological is not the style of coping, but rather the degree to which the defense must be employed in order to avoid confrontation with the stressor. When that becomes so excessive as to destroy the residue of functioning activities, the defense must be considered pathological. But this again raises the question of the criteria for the functioning activity, and who is to determine when an individual is functioning successfully or not—the statistician, the theologian, the physiologist, the humanist. Science is simply not in a position at this point to announce with any degree of certainty when our defenses become pathological.

The critical issue, in fact, may not be the determination of what is pathological at all. A more urgent artistry is demanded of one who would play therapist. Almost anyone can recognize severely pathological defenses against stress. It requires neither great skill nor empathy. It is the property of the callow, insensitive novice to ferret out defenses, and with clinical scalpel in hand, eradicate them in a surgical "search and destroy" mission. To congratulate oneself for acute clinical insight in the wake of such an operation must be a classic exercise of sheer, arrogant sadism. There can be no conceivable value in probing, penetrating and eventually destroying a person's defenses, only to leave the victim with his naked, quivering ego exposed to the conquering view of the therapist. The defenses, after all, are there precisely because the individual needed them; and he needed them because, in his experience at least, he knew of no better way to handle the stress he had experienced. The art of the therapist does not lie in the shrewd discernment of defenses, but in the ability to perceive and educe from the client the self-esteem, sense of value, creativity and resources which he in fact possesses so that he may shuck the defenses at his own pace as scales which have atrophied and died. To this end the therapist works, inviting by his own honesty, candor and power another person to a more productive and open way of coping with stress. Regardless of diagnostic categories, this is the essential art of the therapist. And it is in no sense restricted to those with "credentials." A friend once expressed it to me: "There are times when everyone needs someone to hold his hand. Psychiatrists do this, but never so well as friends."

Notes

1. R. D. Laing, *The Politics of Experience* (New York: Pantheon Books, Inc., 1967), p. 101.
2. *Ibid.*, p. 3.
3. *Cf.* Jan Ehrenwald, *From Medicine Man to Freud* (New York: Dell Publishing Co., Inc., 1956), pp. 114-141.
4. Gregory Zilborg, *History of Medical Psychology* (New York: W.W. Norton & Co., Inc., 1941).
5. Emily Dickinson, *The Poems of Emily Dickinson*, ed. Thomas H. Johnson (Cambridge: The Belknap Press, 1955), Vol. 1, p. 337.
6. Thomas Szasz, *The Myth of Mental Illness* (New York: Harper and Row, 1961).
7. Laing, *op. cit.*, p. 4.

8. Bert Kaplan, ed. *The Inner World of Mental Illness* (New York: Harper & Row, 1964), XII, p. 467.

9. G. B. Levitas, *The World of Psychology,* 2 vols. (New York: George Braziller, Inc., 1963).

10. Silvano Arieti, *The Intra-psychic Self* (New York: Basic Books, Inc., 1967).

11. Laing, *op. cit.*

12. Lawrence C. Kolb, *Noyes' Modern Clinical Psychiatry,* 7th ed. (Philadelphia: W. B. Saunders Co., 1968), pp. 103-104.

13. John C. Nemiah, *Foundations of Psychopathology* (New York: Oxford University Press, 1961), pp. 148-149.

14. Kolb, *op. cit.,* pp. 355-356.

15. Lara Jefferson, "These Are My Sisters," in *The Inner World of Mental Illness,* ed. Bert Kaplan (New York: Harper & Row, 1964), XII, p. 4.

16. Rollo May and others, eds., *Existence* (New York: Basic Books, Inc., 1958).

17. Abraham Maslow, *Toward a Psychology of Being* (Princeton, N.J.: D. Van Nostrand Co., Inc., 1962).

18. Carl Rogers, *On Becoming a Person* (Boston: Houghton Mifflin Co., 1961).

19. Hans Selye, *The Stress of Life* (New York: McGraw-Hill Book Co., 1956).

20. Maslow, *op. cit.,* pp. 19-41.

21. Kurt Lewin, *Dynamic Theory of Personality* (New York: McGraw-Hill Book Co., 1935).

22. Robert Ardrey, *The Territorial Imperative* (New York: Atheneum Publishers, 1966).

23. E. T. Hall, "Territorial Needs and Limits," in *Natural History* (Dec. 1965), pp. 12-19; Ardrey, *op. cit.*

4. Communications:
Clergy and Client

Since 1950, an almost endless series of books has appeared that touched in some way or another on the nebulous subject of pastoral counseling. Most of them featured chapters on the dynamics of homosexuality, or scrupulosity, or alcoholism or any of the other problems which often come to the attention of a pastoral counselor. There have been sections, too, on the techniques of counseling or psychotherapy. However important this information may be, it is simply not the whole story for the counselor. Knowledge is essential, but in this area it is not final. Too often clergy who read these learned chapters felt they were in a position to make clinical judgments about people who came into their office. In doing so, they almost as often lost the person.

In this book, I am primarily concerned about what really happens in the counseling relationship, a transaction between two persons. Research by Eysenck,[1] Alexander and Mendel,[2] Rogers[3] and others has indicated that the words are not the most important element in the counseling relationship. What the patient needs, whatever his pathology, is an experience, not an explanation. He is reaching out for someone, for an experience to counteract hurtful earlier experiences. The clergyman can give him much of that experience. But to do this, he must curtail his manifest tendencies to preach.

As suggested in the previous chapter, the emphasis in abnormal psychology and psychopathology in the past has been upon the diagnosis and cure of a disease in keeping with the classical medical model. We are taught how to recognize the symptoms of an underlying disease, and we are told something about the cure of the sickness. Today, many psychiatrists are asking serious questions about this medical model. Szasz first rejected the medical model of "disease-symptom-diagnosis-cure" as having no real value for psychiatry.[4] We are primarily concerned with the fact that patients are people who are simply not handling themselves satisfactorily in their environment. In this sense, all patients are people; and, to some degree, all people are patients.

Communications Among Clergy

To facilitate communication with our clients it seems evident that we need a good deal more communication among clergy themselves. In fact, what seems to prevent communication with other people, perhaps more than anything else, is the lack of communication among ourselves. Present communication among many clergymen ranges from nothing at all, so that each clergyman in a parish retires to his room or his home and his private television set in the evening, to something of a forced conviviality. We have few close friendships in or out of the clergy. There is a great distance between ourselves and our people, so that as Father Eugene Kennedy remarks, "We can smile innocently and blandly down from a thousand mantlepieces."[5] In some instances there may be a virtual horror of any friendship because of the alleged perversion of particular friendships which was stamped into our minds in seminary days. We are obsessed with the Jansenistic fear of, and the consequent preoccupation with, true friendship.

Our own empirical evidence suggests that there is among the clergy a great hunger for friendship, for genuine communication, a communication which is, basically, the "making-one" with another, being "put-together." First, this means being put together with one's self—a consonance of feeling and thinking, of desiring and action, of saying and doing, a harmony of all the intraorganic systems, intellect, will and emotions, the integration of one's personality, the being real to one's self, the knowledge of *who* I am. All of this is part of intrapersonal communication. There is also a communication with others, an interpersonal communication, a union of feeling and thinking with others, an openness to others. It is a basic axiom that one cannot be open to another unless he is first open to, or one, with himself.

Sending and Receiving

The ingredients of any interpersonal communication are basic and simple. There are two or more persons, and there is a transaction between them. The transaction requires both a sending and a receiving, and it is important to note that *both* are necessary. In the world of communication, we have spent a great deal of time thinking about the sending process but very little time on the receiving process. Yet, *both must be present* for genuine communication. As clergymen, we teach and we preach. We place great importance on this, and we do it almost exclusively. For us, then, how much more important it is to *receive*, to listen for the feedback from our people. We hear thousands of confessions. But how little feedback do we get from what we have said or from the admonitions we have given in confession. Many clergymen seem inclined to say that advice given in a particular situation is right because it is "What I have always told them." There is the danger here of a tyranny of personal expedience, which Abraham Maslow[6] describes in rather classic form when he talks about the psychiatrist who has been making the same mistake for 40 years and calls it rich, clinical experience.

The transaction between people is not only a matter of sending and receiving. It also exists on various levels. There is a verbal level of communication, and there are many non-verbal levels. Words are only one means of communication, and often a poor one, because they can serve as a defense, a barrier to true communication. There can be a dichotomy between what one says and what one does, a lack of integration in the communication. This is exemplified by the old axion "What you are shouts so loudly that I cannot hear what you say." Classically, the difference is exemplified in what we call "content" and "process" in the interpersonal relationship. The *content* is what is said, the words; the *process* is the action that is going on underneath the words, the music. It is essential in counseling to note them both and to note when there is a dichotomy between them.

One sees this dichotomy clearly, for example, in what is called a "smiling depression" in which an individual's bland exterior smile and composure belies the fact that he is crying inside and denying an inner depression for fear of exposure. Or one thinks conversely of the woman who comes into the office looking extremely depressed. In the course of the conversation, she may speak of her husband, insisting that he is quite perfect, a model husband, a good father, an excellent provider, etc. In effect, what she may really be saying beneath the words is, "I hate him because he is so perfect and I am so weak." She would not be so depressed if her husband were as loving as she claims that he is. Or there is the wife who insistently asks her husband, "Do you love me?" To this he will respond, "Yes." Again and again, she might say, "But do you really love me? Do you really love me?" What she really wants to hear unconsciously is, "No." And she will push him until eventually he must satisfy her need to see herself as a martyr, as one who is hurt, as one who is really basically unlovable.

The same sort of thing can happen in a priest-nun relationship, many of which tend to pass under the pretense of some counseling, but in terms of the process are really simply man-woman relationships. We would be much better off if we dealt with them on that level.

Psychic Manipulation

The transaction is an action between persons. There are various models of this. Eric Berne's model outlined in popular form in *Games People Play* ,[7] Everett Shostrom's models in *Man the Manipulator,*[8] are examples of ways in which people work upon one another without saying it. This transaction goes awry when the unconscious or unacknowledged needs of one person speak to the unconscious or unacknowledged needs of the other. This we sometimes refer to as psychic manipulation. It occurs when a suppressed need leaves a quantum of energy unused, and the energy is then displaced in order to maintain organic homeostasis. For example, there may be an unrecognized need to hurt because of a feeling of resentment or hostility against a parent. It is suppressed because this is a bad feeling, and then it appears in compensated form in some prejudice in which an individual can vindicate his own hatred by projecting it upon another person or group. Or it can appear in more subtle forms of torture, as in the tyranny of kindness, in which one tortures others by encumbering them with help in order to serve one's own need to control. We can find it in the evangelist inveighing against sexual practices and ferreting out nefarious acts wherever he can as a compensation for his own preoccupation with sex, a la Elmer Gantry. It is psychic manipulation because it is handling, using or exploiting another person to serve one's own unacknowledged need. There are many forms of psychic manipulation; all of them ruin true communication.

In addition to the *transaction* between the two persons, there are the two persons themselves, or the group which is interacting and the action that is going on within each one, the *intrapersonal* action. It's an axiom here that we can't really play games with one another unless we have first played games with ourself. The person who comes to a pastoral counselor has presumably been playing games with himself. He has, as a consequence, a great many prior feelings already present: his anger, his need for dependence, his need for love, all of which he tends to transfer to the counselor who enters the scene at a late stage of the life drama. If the counselor feels that the feelings are really about him and responds in such a way, he's in a position to be manipulated.

The counselee can also do a good deal of symptom-waving. He can ask the clergyman-counselor to look at him because of his headache, or because he is a good athlete, or because he or she has a problem or because she is sexy. Each is saying, "Don't look at me for myself because I'm afraid that if you really see me, you'll turn away. So look at my symptoms." This symptom-waving is really a way of preserving one's secrecy. Th symptoms must be cleared away in order to get to the underlying dynamics because they can be a mask which the individual must necessarily employ in order to hide himself from what he perceives to be an overwhelming and threatening environment.

There are several things to remark about these symptoms or the games we play with one another. First of all, it must be remembered that the symptom is there for a reason. The individual views himself as weak, bad or helpless, and he sees the environment as overwhelming. He needs to protect himself. It is unwise to nibble away at symptoms unless we are quite sure that we've got something to put in their place. Tearing down symptoms for the pure joy of doing it is a function of amateur psychology. A second caution is that we can be involved in what can easily be a reversal of directions in our thinking about symptoms. The presence of some questionable behavior does not necessarily indicate the presence of a disease. Paranoid people often report that there is someone following them down the street. This does not mean that everyone who says there is someone following him down the street is necessarily a paranoid. A symptom is not a symptom unless there is a disease.

As counselors, we are primarily concerned with the disclosure and elimination of manipulative behavior. We cannot really do much about that in others. We can, however look to ourselves. Thus, the training of mental health workers is now directed more towards the counselor's understanding of himself and his own personal growth rather than to the didactic understanding of the counselee's behavior and dynamics. To open ourselves to others, to get behind the games is a kind of communication that cannot be taught. It is an art.

I cannot speak of the manipulative needs of others. I can, however, speak of my own. I can speak of the actions which in me, as a priest and as a therapist, open the door to psychic manipulation. I recognize in myself a need for power. I am pleased when people ask me to help them. I like it. And because I do, I am ready to be manipulated. The patient who tells me, "I need you" can easily manipulate me. This need for power, I realize, is important. Perhaps what really happens in therapy is the communication of power from the therapist to the patient. But power can also destroy and can create dependence on the part of the counselee. Power destroys when I fail to realize that the therapy is terminated when the patient can say, "I no longer need you." In contrast, I'm also aware of my great feeling of helplessness when dealing with many people. I do not know what to do. I do not know what to offer them. And when we come to that critical moment when the patient asks, "Now what do I do?" I often feel a great surge of hopelessness.

I'm also aware of my being something of a voyeur, a Peeping Tom. I am pleased when secrets are open to me, when I become privy to peoples' individual hang-ups; and I would be less than honest if I did not admit it. Often I am annoyed. I must accept my limitations in this. I can only help those to whom I am honest and open, and, consequently, I must accept my limitations, my annoyance. Should I not acknowledge these feelings in myself, they probably would become evident to the patient in more subtle ways. And he then would have grounds for feeling that I, as others, am also hypocritical and that I am not being honest with him. I often have the feeling of being very threatened. I am threatened by prestige. I need approval from prestige. I can recall working with a professor from a leading university who was clearly more intelligent than I, and I was quite patently threatened by him. I could make no progress therapeutically until I could face the fact that I was threatened by his brilliance and acknowledge it to him. I am challenged or threatened when my power is challenged. When a person comes in and says, "After all, you can't really do anything for me," I want to assure him that I can. If I do, I am manipulated, because he now has my help without even having had to ask for it.

There are many feelings that I have as a priest, too. The first is a feeling of exaggerated responsibility. I must try to help everyone. I have the image of service, of universal accessibility, of being the great and universal helper. C.S. Lewis describes a woman, a social worker, who was noted for her helpfulness. He wrote of her, "You could always tell the people that she helped by their hunted expression."[9] There is a kind of tyranny of kindness when I try to help others in a custodial way. Custody can crush others as surely as hostility does. I feel often that I must help when I cannot. I can easily be manipulated by the person who comes to me and says, "You're my last hope." I wish I could arrive at the point when I could respond by saying, "If I'm your 'last hope,' you had better give up, for I'm not your 'last hope.' You are. God is, but I am not."

I often feel that I must live up to everyone's expectations. I find myself living in terms of others' expectations of me, rather than my own expectations of myself. I sometimes feel I must play the role of the great peacemaker, the great earth mother, suckling all, failing to realize that friction is also good in the interpersonal relationship. On the other hand, I can be a little bit annoyed with the image of myself as a grown-up altar boy. Sometimes, because this image of the priest which I have been given is so impossible to attain, I feel an almost inevitable sense of failure. Because of my failure, I'm afraid that I will retire after 40 to baseball, television and "the plant." And so, I have an unwillingness to fail at all and to admit failure when I'm faced with it. To avoid it, I have a great need to ritualize, to do something, when the counselee asks me. I want to arrange things. This interference at times is necessary. But often the best counseling is done when the counselor is just *there.*

Finally, the most intense form of psychic manipulation occurs when I substitute custody for care. Care lets the other be; custody crushes the other. One of the basic human needs is a certain life space, and it must be preserved.

These forms of manipulation are all modes of an inhuman use of human beings, of the unconscious exploitation of others to satisfy one's own need and in doing so to create irresponsibility in himself and the other. The purpose of counseling is to break through the level of manipulation, to recognize one's needs and be responsible for them and the actions which are consequent upon them. I must learn to let others be. This is the only human use of human beings.

Notes

1. Hans J. Eysenck, *Dimensions of Personality* (London: Kegan Paul, 1955), *passim.*
2. W. Mendel and S. Rapport, "Outpatient Treatment for Chronic Schizophrenic Patients," *Arch. Gen. Psychiat.,* 8 (1963), pp. 190-196.
3. Carl Rogers, *Client-centered Therapy* (Boston: Houghton Mifflin, 1951), pp. 132 ff.
4. Thomas Szasz, *The Myth of Mental Illness* (New York: Harper & Row, 1961).

5. Eugene Kennedy, *Fashion Me a People* (New York: Sheed and Ward, Inc., 1969), pp. 61 ff.

6. Abraham Maslow, *Toward a Psychology of Being* (Princeton, N.J.: D. Van Nostrand Co., Inc., 1962).

7. Eric Berne, *Games People Play* (New York: Grove Press, 1964).

8. Everett Shostrom, *Man, the Manipulator* (Nashville: Abingdon Press, 1967).

9. C. S. Lewis, *The Four Loves* (New York: Harcourt, Brace & World, 1960).

5. *The Clergyman and the Professional Therapist*

In the 1960 Project of Religion and Mental Health at Loyola University of Chicago,[1] four items were stressed as essential to the basic knowledge required of the effective pastoral counselor: first, the ability to recognize the signs of mental illness; second, an understanding of the basic factors of mental health and mental illness; third, some training or savoir faire in counseling; and fourth, a knowledge of community resources and methods of referral. The second and third points have been treated elsewhere in this book. I should like to attend now to the first and the fourth—recognition of the signs of mental illness, and the knowledge of community resources and methods of referral.

The recognition of those emotional problems that one encounters in the rectory, or confessional, or wherever one meets troubled people, seems to be a generally accepted

point of departure. Indeed, it is so basic, and so often bela-
bored that I want to add a particular caution that we do not
turn this process of recognition into some unrelenting witch-
hunt.

Nonetheless, the clergy is in the very front line of the
mental health crusade. Problems come to clergy first. Some
years ago I worked for a period of time in an especially
beleaguered parish in Hollywood, where the number of disturbed people who came through the rectory, and into the
confessionals, reached such alarming size that I thought perhaps the parish itself would be the best place for an emer-
gency clinic.

Symptoms

We ought then to be concerned with the recognition of mental illness, or rather with those signs that tell us that some sort
of psychological malaise is present. Technically we call these
signs "symptoms." Therapy is concerned with dynamics—
the causes, the processes that lie beneath the symptoms. Because we are only concerned with recognition, we are dealing only with the signs or symptoms here.

We must, however, remember that the symptom is not the
whole. It is not the sickness. It is only an expression—a psychological or physiological expression—of a sickness, if there
is such a thing. We can quite easily get so caught up in symptoms that we may lose sight of the sickness itself. A conflict
that we have astutely observed in a person can itself be a
symptom constructed to mask a deeper conflict. The symptom is only a signal by which the person is, perhaps unconsciously, alerting us to the presence of some underlying
conflict.

There is yet another caution. When reading symptoms and
suggesting on the basis of the presence of a symptom that
there is some sort of "illness," one must be very careful of a
reversal of directions. Identical symptomatic behavior can in
different people be an expression of quite different dynamic

conditions. To think that some single sign inescapably suggests the presence of a neurotic process is a presumption that can lead to harmful diagnosis and pseudo treatment.

Neurosis

A number of authors, principally Karen Horney,[2] Harry Stack Sullivan[3] and Robert White[4] have described that basic sequence of psychic events that seems to be involved in the development of any kind of neurosis. One begins with some kind of failure in early personality development. As a consequence of faulty personality development in childhood, the young person develops a depreciative perception of himself. If he has not been loved, then he sees himself as socially inadequate, incompetent. He is afraid. He is so because developmentally, the child's concept of himself is rooted in some identification with the parent and by interiorization of the parent's evaluation of him. So, if the child perceives himself as rejected by the parent, then he sees himself as basically and radically unlovable. This second stage is the core of the neurotic process. If the person sees himself as unlovable and inadequate, then of course everything in the environment becomes a threat, which can overwhelm this weak, inadequate, unlovable self. Everything is awesome, anxiety-producing.

The third stage of the neurotic process follows quite naturally. Karen Horney[5] calls it "basic anxiety," a convenient term for a floating fear, not necessarily attached to any particular object, but the product of the child's perception of itself as inadequate, and therefore easily harmed by any stress in its environment. This anxious, inadequately perceived self *must therefore construct ways of protecting itself against the potentially hostile and threatening environment.* It builds up a protective shell. *These modes of protecting self are what we call defense mechanisms or symptoms of the basic anxiety.*

More technically, the basic free-floating anxiety is defined as a chronic apprehension, with recurring episodes of acute fear, characterized by subjectively felt uneasiness, by the constant anticipation of doom or disaster, by a feeling of helplessness and by a great number of physiological reactions, such as muscular tension, cardiovascular changes, gastro-intestinal problems, sweating, insomnia, irregular breathing, and so on.[6] Neurotic anxiety, or "fear in search of a cause," is said to be free-floating because it isn't attached to any particular object. It is simply the person's overwhelming awareness that he himself is weak, and that, therefore, *anything* in the environment can be threatening to him. He is afraid of it, not because of its own objective threatening value, but because of his own inadequacy and weakness. He must protect this weak self, and he can manage this by constructing all manner of games for coping with the environment.

There are countless defensive modes for coping, or manipulating the environment, or, if you will, symptoms (signs) of the presence of an underlying neurotic process. First, one can present oneself as chronically weak physically, as awfully tired all the time, unable to sleep and very concerned about bodily functions. The person is quite sure that he will suffer appendicitis, cancer or some other unexplained disease. The "neurasthenic" person is actually saying, "Please look at me." He is crying for attention, and he is using physiological weakness to express his underlying feeling of psychological weakness.

Another cluster of symptoms includes the host of so-called hysterical-conversion reactions. Historically, these are among the earliest discerned modes of protecting oneself unconsciously. Freud in his early work dealt largely with hysterical patients and conversion reactions. A psychological malaise is somehow mysteriously converted into physiological symptoms. The sign is clear. There is a physiological sickness without any discernible physiological cause. For example, there are different functional paralyses—those which affect only parts of the body which, in isolation, no extant system of nerves could affect, as in the local paralysis of a part of one's leg. This suggests that the paralysis is not of physiological origin but is a conversion from a psychological sickness.

The conversion can be a sensory one, as in an otherwise inexplicable partial anesthesia. A classic form of this is "glove-anesthesia" where the individual cannot feel anything in his hand approximately in the area that would be covered by a glove. Now, physiologically or neurologically, there is no set of nerves which could possibly explain anesthesia in precisely that area alone, so the cause cannot be neurological. Or the conversion could be a motor symptom. The presence of tremors, of a nervous tic of some sort, a twitch of the head, inexplicable according to muscular structure, indicates the presence of some psychological malaise.

How this conversion from the psychological to the physical takes place, no one is sure, except that here, as in many other cases, *the body is speaking for the psyche.* Many patients will say, for example, "It's awfully difficult to be sick inside and not have anybody see it," or "It is a lot easier to have a broken leg because everybody can see that there is a broken leg and can sympathize." But no one can see a neurosis. So the neurotic's need is precisely to let everybody *see* his sickness. And so mysteriously, via the incomparable body-psyche unit, he unconsciously converts his psychological sickness into a visible, physical one.

Another group of symptoms turns about the various dissociative reactions. One could list here all the amnesia states, the periods of forgetting, "fugue" states, and the multiple personality conditions described so vividly in Cleckley's *Three Faces of Eve.*[7] The individual is dissociated from himself. He's split inside. He is two different people or seems to be. Perhaps he can remember only what one of his "persons" and not what another "person" has done.

Still another form of symptom formation is the phobic reaction. The characteristic is that the phobia, or fear, is unreasonable and disproportionate. The individual is afraid of cats, or mice, or a bird, or something which is really not a fearsome object. The free-floating fear of the basic anxiety is now, by means of some conditioning or association, attached to a particular object, so that the individual can unconsciously tell himself, "*This* is the reason why I am afraid." This, too, is a very early recorded mode of defense in the history of psychiatric diagnosis. Freud in 1909 described, in the case of *Little Hans,* [8] the chronicle of a boy who was afraid of horses. The horse, as Freud described it in this classical case, was associated with the boy's father, and the boy's fear of his father had been converted to fear of the horse. There can be, of course, as many phobias as there are objects to be afraid of. The list is dull and interminable: claustrophobia, the fear of enclosed or small places; agoraphobia, the fear of open spaces; melissaphobia, the fear of bees; gephyraphobia, the fear of crossing water; parthenophobia, the fear of virgins; and even homilophobia, the fear of sermons. Whatever can be said of such a directory of terms, each describes a symptom and not the real fear. And it is useless to try to argue the individual out of this strange, exotic, conditioned fear.

The process of symptom formation can also be observed in obsessive-compulsive reactions, or the tendency to repeat the same act over and over again. An individual may need to count telephone poles, or wash his hands, or confess some trivia, or whatever. It is the "Lady Macbeth" syndrome. The individual can assure you very definitely that he doesn't know why he's doing it, but he simply must. The clergyman in his parlor or confessional is often confronted with some such psychological problem in religious clothing. The problems of *scruples* or *masturbation* fall into this part of the mosaic. The clinical picture of the obsessive-compulsive presents us with a person who is very indecisive because of his feeling of personal worthlessness, and he handles his felt worthlessness by ritual compensation. He makes up for his inadequacy by the repetition of symbolic acts, and through the magical force of the acts he brings order into his life.

The last type of symptom that I'd like to mention is the

depressive reaction. Once called "melancholia" by the ancients, it is probably the oldest category in the annals of psychiatric literature. Freud entitled one of his most significant essays *Mourning and Melancholia.*[9] In it, he distinguished normal grief from pathological depression. The depressed person exhibits a good deal of insomnia, unexplained fits of crying, occasional failures of memory, diminished activity, inability to get interested in anything, dysphoria and a bland, indifferent feeling-tone. In the depressive patient, the anger and resentment about feeling inadequate is turned in on himself, and the depression is the effect of this introjected hostility.

There are many other patterns of symptom formation, but these, I think, give one a broad and nominal overview of the signs that suggest that some neurotic process is at work. When a cluster of these signs are encountered, the individual should be referred to a competent psychotherapist.

Psychosis

So far, we have considered neurotic development only, as opposed to rather more gross symptomatology of a psychotic flavor. Actually, the dynamic process is somewhat the same. There is at root, again, some faulty personality development. But in the psychotic reaction, the individual, instead of constructing defenses for his inadequacy against a threatening environment, finds one or another way to withdraw from the environment into an inner world of fantasy and illusion.

The neurotic process is, after all, familiar. It is easy to understand because all of us are more or less neurotic and anxious, and all of us do construct different selves, different faces or defenses to protect ourselves. The difference is only one of degree. But the psychotic reaction is *not* familiar. It is incomprehensible. It is illogical. It is unreal and bizarre and weird. Basically, the psychotic reaction is the loss of the ego control so important to us. For Freud, the ego was the mediating force between demands of the id and pressures of the environment. Ego provided the self-control that made it possible for one to live in a society that didn't always yield to its needs. In the psychotic, this ego control is lost. The individual has withdrawn into an interior world. There is no reality testing, little distinction between the self and the other and loss of thought control. Such ego loss can be effected either by a psychotic withdrawal, by drug intervention, as in some psychedelic experiences, or indeed by meditation. The mystics experienced something of a loss of ego control. So the schizophrenic psychotic reaction and the psychedelic experience are often thought to be somewhat mystical in character. However fascinating this similarity is, ego loss itself is not the point here. The point in the psychotic flight is the inability to regain ego control.

Among the indices of an unredeemable loss of ego control is the presence of hallucinations, perceptions without external stimuli. The internal stimulus is thought by the individual to be external, a confusion made possible by the ego loss of which we spoke. The hallucinations that are statistically most common are auditory in nature, usually voices. One hears voices in the ventilating system, or walls, or in the glove compartment of the car. Edgar Allen Poe's story *The Tell-Tale Heart*, in which a murderer heard the beating of the heart of the cadaver that he had buried under the floor, is an example of an auditory hallucination. The second most common are the visual hallucinations—the perception of a spider on the wall, or a pink elephant, etc., presented so dramatically in *The Lost Weekend*. Common, too, in the psychotic reaction are tactual hallucinations—the feeling of the D.T.'s. The schizophrenic, for example, often feels that his body is infested with crawling things.

Somewhat similar dynamically to hallucinations, though not perceptual in nature, are delusions. We described hallucinations as percepts without external stimuli. Delusions are concepts without external verification. They may indeed have many different subjects, but they usually concern the self and turn about concepts of one's own omnipotence, or one's grandeur. The individual may think that he is the president of the university, or a great inventor, or vocalist or whatever. They are also said to be ideas of reference when the individual has the feeling that everyone is thinking about him, or acting on him in some way, or if he has ideas of persecution or hypochondriacal delusions. These can flower to the degree that one feels his body is decaying. Both hallucinations and delusions are the signs of the presence of some schizophrenic process in the perceptual-cognitive orders, respectively.

But there are other, more subtle, signs of the withdrawal process. First of all, the schizophrenic in the early stages manifests a loss of interest in the environment, a detachment, a dearth of emotional response, a kind of blandness about his behavior. At yet another stage, he can become very preoccupied or obsessed with a special problem or idea. He may think about nothing other than the war in Vietnam. There is no flexibility in his thinking. He cannot be distracted from talking about the war in Vietnam. The phenomenon in question here is not the validity or importance of the idea, but his preoccupation with it. This obsession also indicates that in the process of ego loss the individual has ceased to check his thinking against the environment outside, and therefore he cannot shift from one thought to another. Once the thought is paramount in his mind, it sticks there, a phenomenon described by Kurt Goldstein as "concrete concept-formation."[10] The symbol has ceased to be a symbol and has become an entity in itself.

There is also a stage in the schizophrenic process when the individual experiences a kind of anxiety. It's not the same as the basic anxiety of the neurotic process, but rather a specific fear that he may lose his mind. He panics at the thought and becomes at the same time preoccupied with it.

These are but a few of the danger-signals suggesting to a clergyman that he should try to refer the person for professional psychiatric or psychological care. We ought now to be concerned about how he goes about doing that—*the mechanics of the referral.*

The Referral Process

It is important to note at the very beginning that the *referral process itself is part of the therapy* because it, too, is essentially a relationship between one person in need and another helping person. It is not sufficient to detect with prideful acuity that an individual is sick and then tell him bluntly, "Man, you had better see a psychiatrist." It is not enough simply to call a psychiatrist and get the patient to him. This should be an ongoing relationship. The clergyman is obliged in the whole of the referral process to continue, insofar as he can, with the psychiatrist and with the family of the patient.

The first step in the referral process is, of course, to know when to refer and to whom. The clergyman must have somewhere in his working library a directory that will help him to locate quickly those agencies for people in need of psychotherapeutic care. One should also have some professional relationship with one or more individual psychiatrists or psychologists with whom he carries on referral work. The relationship often becomes a very warm and close one.

One hazard we ought to avoid in the referral process is the genuine likelihood of being manipulated by the patient. After all, for most patients, it's a lot nicer to see a clergyman than it is to see a psychiatrist. And so long as they can, many would like to hang on to the illusion that theirs is a spiritual problem and not a psychological one. There is always the tendency on the patient's part to try to cleanse himself of his own humanity. Or there is the tendency to move from one cleric to another, to try to hang on to each one and to gain his sympathy and attention until the point of weakness that the individual is trying to protect is finally reached. They will come to you and say, "You're the only priest or minister that I've ever been able to confide in. I saw so-and-so, but he didn't help me." All of these are attempts to hang on.

There are lots of difficulties that one encounters in the referral process, too. You will meet the person who says, "But I don't want to see a psychiatrist," or "I don't have any money," or "I don't need to be referred. This is a religious problem." Or he may say, "I am not mentally ill," or "I am afraid of shock-therapy," or "I'm afraid of what they'll do to me," or "I'm afraid for my job and my family." These are most frequently veiled attempts to cling to a relationship which he or she perceives to be much less threatening than that of the patient with the psychiatrist.

For this reason, I suggest that it is very important when making a referral *to contact personally and directly the therapist* to whom you are referring the patient. If he is a psychiatrist, call him. Work out with him a way of overcoming these difficulties in referral and a way of sustaining the relationship with the patient and with the psychiatrist after treatment has begun. Community work is intensely important. The same is true of the clinics to which one might refer a patient—*call them first!* Establish a relationship with them.

There is also that chronic question of whether or not one should refer to a psychiatrist of the same faith as the patient. For me the only answer to this question is a very simple one. We do not refer to a Catholic psychiatrist, or to a Protestant psychiatrist, or to a Jewish psychiatrist, *but to a good one.* Other qualities are not relevant to therapy. Nor do we refer a patient to him because he is necessarily smarter, but because he simply has a bigger bag of tricks from which he can draw to help the individual recover his equilibrium.

Finally, there are, I believe, times when the clergyman should *not* refer. We said previously that a symptom is not a symptom unless there is some underlying disease. Similar behavior in two persons, therefore, can be symptomatic in one and yet not in another. Two *dynamically different* phenomena can look very much alike in the symptomatic level. For example, the asceticism of the saints can look like the masochism of the neurotic, and the desolation described in the manuals of the spiritual life can look like neurotic depression. This does not mean they are the same; but differentiating between them can be a very delicate job. Historically, the tendency has been to make a cavalier solution by simply denying the dilemma and reducing all symptoms to one universal explanation. All asceticism, therefore, is said to be nothing but an expression of some underlying masochism; or conversely, all forms of penance are said to be truly saintly asceticism. In this regard, I would like to suggest that it is the function largely of the clergy to distinguish between these conditions. This is an enormous and critical area in the relationship between psychology and ascetical theology, and we will return to it in the next chapter.

The clergyman probably should also not refer when the case is considered to be one that is accessible to pastoral counseling. In this respect, we are all counselors concerned with what goes on between ourselves, the person and God in the pastoral counseling relationship.

The first ingredient, of course, in the relationship between the clergyman and his parishoner is the presence of *rapport*, a genuine personal, empathetic relationship. Unfortunately, this has come to be something of a magic word. And we are prone sometimes to reify rapport, to make a *thing* out of it. The phrase "to establish rapport" often has the unfortunate connotation of making something, as one might make pies or puddings. But we simply can't make rapport. It is above all real, and any attempts to create it by practicing some sort of ritual, like offering a client a cigarette, or affecting a bland smile or tendering a brief but meaningful squeeze on the elbow are bound to fail. *The patient,* the parishoner, *is in need.* He needs *reality, not tokens.* For the counselor, the only valid criterion for the establishment of rapport is: does he want to be with this person? If he does, then he will have rapport, and it will be therapeutic. For above all, the person, the client, needs a friend. And it is the function of the therapist, be he priest or professional therapist, to be a friend. This is the essential element. The element that allows transference is the one that makes therapy possible. Regardless of the enormous range of problems that the priest or minister may face, to each new encounter he must bring the same personal qualifications. In the final analysis, counseling rests upon the person-to-person interaction. Nothing can substitute for this personal dimension. We are tempted to search for techniques that can be sorted out and applied discriminately to each distinct problem, yielding a specific remedy for a specific malaise. But there are no techniques, no formulae, no pat solutions. It is not the technique that cures, but the human experience in which the client and the counselor will grow. Viktor Frankl, the Austrian existential psychiatrist, remarks that "worshipping techniques at the expense of encounter involves making man not only a mere thing, but a means to an end, and that is the same as manipulating him."[11]

For there to be such an encounter, the first indispensable function of the priest-counselor is that he *listen.* And here we risk the use of what often seems to be another magic word. Despite all that has been said about listening, it is still rare. We have watched little children at play, chattering with one another, with not the least sign of communication. Indeed, if one of the children were removed, the other in all likelihood would continue his chatter with no discernible change. Piaget calls this "collective monologues." Children by necessity talk to themselves. Adults do it by choice. Our communications media, for example, seem jammed with noises, but with no proportionate amount of listening. Yet communication is nothing without listening. If the clergyman can bring to this human encounter a real receptivity, it may be the first time in his life that the parishoner has ever really communicated. It may be the first time that anyone has really listened to him, and in this experience he will grow. As a listener, the clergyman is accessible. He is *there* to the client.

Every disturbed person, regardless of his presenting problem, is somehow, as we indicated before, *not* in the world. The schizophrenic has abdicated from the world in favor of a world of fantasy and symbol. The slightly neurotic is suffering an incalculable urge to run from the world, to defend and protect himself from its threats and to construct what Karen Horney calls the "phony-self in a phony-world."[12] Each of them is not quite properly in the world, and it is the contribution of the counselor by his presence, by his being there, to witness to that real world for the client, to induce him to re-enter it and thus to realize his unique place in the world. For each disturbed person has in some way lost his bearings, his place. He is as one in the dark in a strange room feeling his way, bumping into one object, and then another and being hurt. He is deathly afraid of that hurt. To rid himself of it he needs to do one thing: run the risk, expose himself in all his fancied nothingness to another and be accepted by him. In the counseling relationship between the pastor and his disturbed parishioner, there can ensue this real healing encounter. Gabriel Marcel calls it "the meeting of two persons, in which each awakens to the presence of the other and in so doing reveals his own presence to the other."[13]

This presence to the client is another way of saying that the pastor-counselor himself is exposed to, is opened to, indeed, *loves* the client. Clergymen tend sometimes to live in a world of magic, ritual and secrecy. Because of this tendency we may be much less accessible to our people. Our openness to our people is the therapeutic agent of total importance. It is our aim that those persons who present themselves, often at great costs, to the pastor-counselor for care because they are alien to themselves can become present to another, and by that act can become present to themselves and to God.

Notes

1. *Report on Project of Religion and Mental Health* (Chicago: Loyola Univ. Press, 1961).
2. Karen Horney, *Neurosis and Human Growth* (New York: W.W. Norton & Co., 1950), p. 13ff.
3. Harry Stock Sullivan, *Clinical Studies in Psychiatry* (New York, W.W. Norton & Co., 1956), pp. 3-37.

4. Robert White, *The Abnormal Personality* (New York: The Ronald Press Co., 1956), chap. 5.
5. Horney, *op. cit.,* pp. 18, 287, *passim.*
6. Rollo May, *The Meaning of Anxiety* (New York: The Ronald Press Co., 1950), chaps. 3, 4; Isidore Portnoy, "The Anxiety States," in *American Handbook of Psychiatry* (New York: Basic Books Inc., 1959), Vol. 1, pp. 307-323.
7. Hervey M. Cleckley and Corbett H. Thigpen, *The Three Faces of Eve* (New York: McGraw-Hill, 1957).
8. Sigmund Freud, *Collected Papers,* ed. Ernest Jones (London: Hogarth, 1948), Vol. 3, pp. 149-288; Ernest Jones, *The Life and Work of Sigmund Freud* (New York: Basic Books Inc., 1955), p. 260.
9. *Ibid., Mourning and Melancholia, Collected Papers,* ed. E. Jones (London: Hogarth, 1948), Vol. 2, pp. 152-172.
10. Kurt Goldstein, *Human Nature in the Light of Psychopathology* (Cambridge: Harvard Univ. Press, 1947), p. 59ff.
11. Viktor Frankl, *The Doctor and the Soul* (New York: Alfred A. Knopf, 1963).
12. Horney, *op. cit.,* pp. 21-23.
13. Gabriel Marcel, *The Existential Background of Human Dignity* (Cambridge: Harvard Univ. Press, 1963).

PRACTICE

6. *A Case for Pastoral Psychology: Depression or Desolation*

Theology and spiritual direction, psychology and psycho-therapy have complementary quests. Both seek to define and inspire a sense of life and its meaning; both are directed to the development and maturity of the whole man. Yet, there are differences between them in methods and in tradition, and out of these differences stormy conflicts have arisen with predictable regularity. In the atmosphere of conflict both sides were inclined to explain all relevant phenomena in terms of their own discipline exclusively. The psychologist saw all forms of spiritual asceticism as nothing but gratifying forms of narcissistic exhibitionism. Freud spoke of God as a cultural father image, and the Eucharist as a primitive kind of oral cannibalism. Spiritual directors, on the other hand, were often too ready to explain pathological conditions in terms of mystical experience, signs of divine predilection.

Hagiographers of the past not infrequently attributed supernatural explanations to phenomena which could have been
explained by natural causes. Visions, cures, levitations and
stigmata were unquestioningly reported as of divine origin,
when they were, in fact, cases of hysterical conversion reaction. Either mode of interpretation is guilty of reductionism.

   In the tugging back and forth of the conflict, the pendulum
has swung erratically. No self-respecting spiritual director
would have considered referring a young religious to a psychiatrist 25 years ago, but such referrals have now become
more the rule than the exception. Clergy seem more than
ready now to explain mysterious events as coincidences in-
duced by a subtle collaboration of natural causes and to be
apologetic of their ascetical tradition, possibly because they
have never opened themselves to mystical experiences or
even believed them possible.

Spiritual Desolation

As a case in point, there is the perplexing differential diagnosis between the neurotic depressive reaction and what ascetical writers have consistently described as spiritual
desolation. Since the beginning of the study of psychopathology, there has been an abundance of research, clinical experience and theory on states of depression. On the other hand,
since the time of the Fathers of the Church in the third and
fourth centuries after Christ an even longer tradition among
spiritual writers described a stage of development in prayer
and the spiritual life called desolation, aridity, the dark night
of the senses, etc. The first state is said to be pathological; the
second is said to be of divine origin. To be sure, there are
great resemblances between the descriptions of the two
phenomena. In each there is the experience of great sadness,
a feeling of loss, an emotional flatness, motor retardation,
insomnia, etc. On these symptomatic grounds alone, psychologists assumed that there was some underlying pathology; while theologians with equal authoritativeness

insisted that the symptoms were signs of divine predilection. In the face of this massive noncommunication, it is difficult to determine whether there is only one kind of experience, differently described by authors with different prejudices, or two distinct kinds of experience, confused because of their symptomatic similarity.

There has been a long-standing attempt, at least among the spiritual writers and some psychologists, to identify and distinguish the two states. Lot-Borodine[1] compiled selections from many ancient authors who spoke of two kinds of "sadness" as early as the third and fourth century. He reviews this history through the works of Clement of Alexandria and Origen, and finds testimony also in the work of St. Augustine,[2] who himself spoke of bitterness, a pathological condition, and sadness, a stage of spiritual progress. In the famous fifteenth century spiritual manual *The Practice of Perfection and Christian Virtues,* Rodriguez writes:

> . . . St. Basil says, and St. Leo Pope, and Cassian also mentions it, that there are two sorts of sadness. One is worldly, when one is sad for something of the world, its adversities and troubles; and that sadness they say the servants of God ought not to have. . . . Another sadness there is that is spiritual and according to God, good and profitable, and becoming the servants of God.[3]

Grimbert highlights the problem for the diagnostician:

> It is both legitimate and most important to ask whether one is able to infer a similarity of symptoms throughout the mental or moral depressions, or whether there is not a certain class of illness, which suggests to us, after ruling out manifest psychopathology, a real example (and not just a simple copy) of the dryness of the soul encountered on the pathways of the spiritual ascent.[4]

The difficulty lies, of course, in identifying that certain class. In 1937, Allers focused on the problem directly when he spoke of symptomatic and dynamic aridity.

I mean to indicate by these two states of soul which so resemble each other that they may very well be of strongly different origin. The symptomatic "aridity" is truly a symptom, part of an ensemble of traits which are more or less pathological. The dynamic "aridity" is a phase of development of the interior life.[5]

Despite such recognition and clear statement of the problem, it has not been studied much. One finds the usual lack of communication between the two disciplines of ascetical theology and clinical psychiatry and the consequent use of two entirely different vocabularies. Grimbert[6] noted this language barrier in 1937 and proposed that it was the reason for the absence of any real studies.

Historically, some suggestions have been made regarding diagnostic signs which could be employed to distinguish the two states. The fifth century Abbot, Cassian, offered a sample catalogue of signs:

> ... by which we may know what sadness is good and according to God, and what is evil. He says that the former is obedient, affable, meek, gentle, and patient. . . . But the evil sadness . . . is rude, impatient, full of resentment and fruitless bitterness, inclining to diffidence and despair, and withdrawing and removing from all good.[7]

The more productive approach, however, has been to try to see the two phenomena in the context of the individual's total life picture, to judge the nature of the depression from that total picture, and not just on the presence or absence of certain signs. This differentiation can best be made by viewing the ensemble of characteristics in the light of the overall direction of an individual's life. But a diagnosis in terms of the life picture can only be determined, as Allers has noted, *a parte post*,[8] and is, therefore, of little value to the diagnostician who is obliged to render a decision in the present without waiting for the testimony of an individual's complete life. He concludes by noting that there has not been enough research as yet to provide us with a valid diagnostic criterion.

And that is the object of this chapter: to study the problem of a differential diagnostic between spiritual desolation and the neurotic depressive reaction from the point of view of psychology. The ascetical tradition suggests that two such dynamically distinct states do in fact exist, and each should be differentiated. And this belief offers the first formulation of a theory: Spiritual desolation and the neurotic depressive reaction are symptomatically alike but dynamically distinct. The first step in the examination of the theory is a more studied review of the two phenomena involved.

The Neurotic Depressive Reaction

Clinical descriptions of depressive states can be found as early as the writings of Hippocrates, who in the fourth century B.C. attributed them to the presence of black bile and phlegm affecting the brain. Aretaeus of Rome in the first century A.D. wrote of melancholia in a manner not unlike the sophisticated psychiatric literature of the first half of this century. Significant attempts to refine the concept began with Meyer,[9] who eliminated the term "melancholia" in favor of "depression" in 1907. And Kraepelin[10] in 1909 pointed out the need to differentiate the depressive reaction as a specifically discrete clinical entity from the depressive psychoses. This recognition led to the ultimate adoption of the category "reactive depression," as a subdivision of the psychoneuroses.

Since Kraepelin, there have been innumerable attempts to classify the syndrome precisely. In 1952 Ascher reviewed seven classifications extant at that time, and there have been many more.[11] The War Department classification of 1945[12] popularized the designation "Neurotic depressive reaction," which was subsequently adopted in the nomenclature approved by the American Psychiatric Association in 1952.[13] According to this classification, there are six classes of depression:

1. Manic-depressive reaction, depressive type
2. Manic-depressive reaction, other (specified) type
3. Psychotic depressive reaction
4. Involutional depressive reaction
5. Schizophrenic reaction, schizo-affective type
6. Neurotic depressive reaction

The only one of these classifications to be considered in this chapter is the neurotic depressive reaction. Since 1952, less emphasis has been placed on the classification of depressive states, and where they are still used the nomenclature of the American Psychiatric Association's classification is usually the most common.

Symptoms

According to the War Department's original classification, the neurotic depressive reaction differs from psychotic depression in degree and in the absence of gross misinterpretations of external reality. It is characterized by self-depreciation, the introjection of feelings and by guilt feelings. It is precipitated by some loss, and it is generally related to repressed aggression. Jaeger notes that the term "reactive depression" is applied "... when an external cause, such as business failure, social failure, disappointment in love, the death of a loved one precipitates the depression."[14] In the *American Handbook of Psychiatry*, Gutheil describes the neurotic depressive reaction as "... an acute feeling of despondency and dysphoria of varying intensity and duration ... a response to conditions of loss and disappointment."[15] He outlines the symptoms as diminished activity, lowered self-assurance, apprehension, constricted interests and loss of initiative with feelings of weakness and helplessness. The world seems to threaten his depreciated self-esteem. The feeling is often accompanied by overcompensated ambition and the necessity to fail. Cleghorn and Curtis support the War Department's classification in noting that the reactive depressive, in contrast to the endogenous or psychotic depressive, whose illness is of bodily origin and a fundamental, lasting derangement, does not show major personality disorganization or falsifications of reality such as delusions or hallucinations.[16] The personality organization is frequently of the conscientious, obsessive-compulsive type, although hysterical patterns are also seen.

In cases of the neurotic depressive reaction, the precipitating stress is usually identifiable, but seems to be inadequate to elicit the serious degree of mood change which occurs with the concomitant reports of worthlessless, inferiority and depreciation. Such persons turn mainly to the environment and display powerful strivings for security, as well as a definite hunger for love. They want the environment to assure them that they are not as unworthy and unlovable as they report. Failures here will be accompanied by distressing subjective ambivalence, inhibition and loss of energy. Complaints of internal emptiness, inhibition and drive decreases are common. Freud found that the depressive reaction accompanied the loss of a loved object.[17] The depressed person feels a painful rejection, inhibition of interest in the outside world, loss of the capacity to love and a lowering of self-regarding feelings to a degree that self-reproaches and self-revilings culminate in the expectation of punishment and doom. Freud believed that these self-accusations were actually reproaches against the loved object shifted to the patient's own ego.

In their monumental efforts to present an aggregate picture of the depressive symptomatology, the authors of the *Minnesota Multiphasic Personality Inventory* collected a comprehensive listing of symptoms that the depressed patient is likely to display.[18] On the physical side, they include anorexia (loss of appetite), insomnia, fits of crying, memory failures, feeling of general weakness, hypertension and general hypochondriacal concern. The depressed patient is usually sad, given to feelings of failure and rejection, hypersensitive, brooding, fearful, withdrawn and despairing.

Because of indifference, disinterest and a certain impairment of intellectual acuity, his work also suffers. And these symptoms are set against a pervading lack of self-confidence and a tendency to self-depreciation.

Dynamics

Cleghorn and Curtis state that there are three opinions with respect to the etiology of reactive depression. One theory holds that whereas the endogenous depression is somatogenic, i.e., it develops from within the body, the reactive depression is psychogenic (of mental or emotional origin). The second opinion is that all depression, regardless of classification, is psychogenic in nature. And a third maintains that all depressions are the result of the interplay of different processes, of the interaction, that is, between heredity and the early and late environment. In support of the constitutional predisposition, many psycho-physiologists have argued that the exaggerated and prolonged reaction to some unpleasant experience, characteristic of the depressive, is inexplicable apart from the presence of constitutional factors. But most agree that there is a psychic predisposition as well. In a study of reactive depressives, it was found that 74 per cent were sensitive, insecure, serious, withdrawn, shy personalities with a pedantic love of order and a tendency to work through their experiences internally.[19] Twelve per cent were inclined to be disgruntled, obstinate, irritable people, with a tendency to react violently and to feel grossly misunderstood. Ten per cent were predominantly schizoid personalities. And four per cent were sociable and extroverted.

Among the purely psychogenic interpretations, the psychoanalytic schools provide the greatest variety of theories. Freud believed that the self-torments experienced by the depressed patient are actually expressions of hate directed at the original object choice.[20] This original object choice, selected on a narcissistic basis, proves injurious or disappointing; but rather than withdraw the libido from the subject, the individual introjects it. Thus, the melancholic is fixated at the primitive level of oral, narcissistic introjection, which accounts for his great dependency. Karl Abraham also stressed the factors of hostility and orality as essential to the depressive states, and felt, as a result, that the depression was the result of very early disappointments in the child's relationship to his parent.[21] These early disappointments seem to consist of situations in which the child shatteringly discovers that he is not his mother's favorite, or not really loved by her at all. On occasions of subsequent disappointments, the child finds that his love is so overwhelmed by hate that he abandons the object as something distasteful and disgusting, and then introjects it into his own ego and becomes narcissistically identified with the hated object. This hostility which is now self-directed becomes the object of self-reproach. Therefore, Abraham postulated that the depressive's self-reproaches and self-criticism were really directed against the lost love object. Melanie Klein pushed the area of analytical interest back to the infant's first year of life and postulated the processes of introjection and projection at this early stage.[22] For Klein, the depressive predisposition depended on the quality of the mother-child relationship and the frustrations resultant upon the loss of the first love objects.

Jacobsen considered rather that the depression was intimately linked with the loss of self-esteem.[23] When the ego-ideal is for some reason unattainable, there follows an aggressive cathexis (holding fast) of the self-image. In addition, the depressive has early experienced such disappointments that he feels unvalued, unwanted, and sustains a deep narcissistic injury, the result of an introjection of parental judgments. This narcissistic injury interferes with both the optimal self-cathexis and adequate object representations. These object representations are insufficiently separated from the parental component of the self-ideal, and therefore, they are unrealistically idealized. The patient feels himself dependent upon them all, and this dependency leads in turn to intolerance to hurt, frustration, disappointment. The defenses or denial, or the rationalized inadequacy of the love object keeps the depressive in the dependent position, concealing his own intrinsic worth and contributing to the tendency to see self as weak and helpless. Cameron sees the depressive reaction as organized around an unconscious sense of guilt, the result of excessive hostility.[24] He feels that the excessive dependency needs stem rather from rewarding love relationships in childhood that must always have seemed in danger of disappearing. Love was never unconditional, but always dependent upon submission. This continues, so that as an adult the depressive must constantly insure a continual supply of love and support, or at least envy and admiration. While he can do nothing that risks forfeiting this attention and striving for achievement, he resents his emotional dependence and hates the people whom he must always please.

While differing in specific aspects of their theories, the psychoanalytic writers agree in basic outline. The personality structure of the depressive is marked by defenses of introjection, dependency, a severely critical superego, unconscious hostility turned inwards and low self-esteem. These center around the real or perceived loss of a love object. The hostility towards the love object, who has disappointed him in an early love relationship, is introjected and produces the severe superego, guilt feelings and a conviction of worthlessness. The attempt to win back the lost love object produces the dependency and subsequent disappointments trigger the depressive reaction.

The Spiritual Desolation

In both the Western and Eastern Church traditions, cases of spiritual desolation have been described from earliest times. "Desolation" was derived from the Greek word "penthos." And that state is described by Cyril of Philea as "... a sadness sent by God"[25] and by Gregory Nyssa as ". . . a mournful disposition of the soul, caused by the loss of something desirable."[26] Hausherr reviewed this entire tradition in the *Orien-*

talia Christiana Analecta in which he noted the universality of the tradition and substantiated his claim with innumerable citations from the writings of Clement of Alexandria, Origen, the Cappadocians, John Chrysostom and others.[27] Martin, in 1957, in the *Dictionnaire de Spiritualité*, stated that the same tradition was as prevalent in the West, and wrote that ". . . all periods of Christian hagiography offer examples of spiritual desolation."[28] He found testimony in the works of Diadocus of Photia, in the *Spiritual Ladder* of John Climacus, who spoke of desolation as "compunctio cordis," in the conferences of the Abbot Cassian and others. Rodriguez quotes the same Cassian as having said that: "Persons of great merit and wisdom sometimes abandon themselves so far to this deep melancholy to cry like children, or when they feel the melancholy coming, to shut themselves in their chambers where they may be at liberty to weep."[29] Moving to relatively more modern testimony, Martin also reviewed seven case studies of spiritual desolation, in the lives of John of the Cross, Jean de Jesus-Marie, Jeanne de Chantal, Paul of the Cross, Alphonsus Liguori, Emile de Rodat and St. Theresa.

So extensive was the tradition that a number of spiritual classics were devoted exclusively to it. *The Cloud of Unknowing*, an anonymously written fourteenth century English classic, stresses the uncertainty and blindness that afflict the men of faith.[30] Dom Knowles claims that the "cloud" corresponds to the dark night, described by John of the Cross. In 1647, Louis Chardon published *La Croix de Jesus*,[31] in which he attempted to describe the whole of the spiritual life in terms of desolation, as did Baker in *The Great Desolation*,[32] published in 1876. Rudolf Allers, Bruno de Jesus-Marie[33] and others have brought the tradition up to date by reviewing, in different collections, a number of contemporary case studies. Testimony, then, is not wanting to the effect that the tradition describing the spiritual desolation is a long and consistent one.

As in the case of the neurotic depression, such an ubiquitous and variously described phenomenon is in need of more

precise classification. Martin and Daeschler, in the *Dictionnaire de Spiritualité,*[34] provide the following list of categories: "distaste," "aridity," "the Great Desolation," "the
Common Desolation." "Distaste" is a general term to describe any feelings of repugnance for the things of God. Daeschler defines "aridity" as "... a state in which the soul feels
an impotence, or at least great difficulty, in producing acts
proper to prayer."[35] Louis de la Trinite notes that the word
"aridity" etymologically means to be dry, to lack the irriga-
tion that turns the arid soil fertile, and thus it suggests the
image of a "desert," the frequent habitat for the monks who
often wrote of the state.[36] As such, "aridity" is specifically a
state of prayer, and should not be confused with desolation,
which is a condition affecting the whole of the spiritual life.
The two kinds of desolation differ, according to Martin, only
in degree. "The great desolation" describes a persistent and
grave state in which the person feels that he has fallen, without knowing how, into disgrace before God. And this corresponds to the dark night of the soul in the classification of
John of the Cross. "The common desolation" is a less intense
suffering and, again according to Martin, is common to all the
just. To it corresponds the dark night of the senses, described
by John of the Cross.

Symptoms

As in all cases of depression or desolation, "the common
desolation" is characterized by a sense of loss. In this instance, it is the feeling of the loss of the presence of God.
Angela de Foligno is quoted as saying of her desolation:
"... I find myself tormented; and it seems to me that I can
feel nothing about God, and that I have been abandoned by
Him."[37] The sense of loss, in this case the painful feeling of
the loss of God, literally a hell, is the chief characteristic of
both depression and desolation. Accompanying the sense of
loss are the usual overt depressive symptoms. There are feelings of dryness of sensibility, doubts, inquietude, inertia,

revulsion, a darkening of the intellect and despair. One feels alone, isolated. In that loneliness, prayer becomes impossible, faults are magnified, there is disdain for the things of God, as well as for all created things, and the self-depreciating feeling that one is, and should be, disdained by God. Jean de Jesus-Marie likened his desolation to that of one who is locked in prison, unable to pray, feeling distaste for everything and at the same time anxious about his salvation.[38] Jeanne de Chantal described the physical reactions when she noted that ". . . one also loses the desire to drink, eat, or sleep."[39] There is a feeling of indifference about the self, the environment and God for which the individual feels a terror of Divine Justice, a subjective conviction that God will surely convict him of innumerable sins. St. Ignatius summarized the experience:

> I call by the name of desolation that darkness and confusion of soul, attraction to base objects, disquietude caused by various agitations and temptations which make the soul distrustful, without hope or love, so that it finds itself altogether slothful, tepid, sad, and as it were, separated from its Creator and Lord.[40]

The final authority in any matters concerning the phenomenon of desolation is John of the Cross. In two works, *The Ascent of Mount Carmel*[41] and *The Dark Night of the Soul*,[42] he describes the symptoms, offers diagnostic signs, outlines the dynamics and etiology and gives direction concerning what the person passing through such a stage should do. He outlines the stages of spiritual development according to six steps. First, one is totally devoted to sensible satisfactions, to need-gratification. From this stage, the person is weaned by means of the dark night of the senses, and prepared for a higher spiritual maturity. And this is the second stage. It is important for the purpose of this study to draw attention to the fact that this night of the senses, or "common desolation," is not an infrequent phenomenon. John of the Cross states specifically that it is ". . . common and comes to many; these are the beginners. "Ordinarily, no great time passes after their beginnings before they begin to enter this night of the senses; and the great majority of them do in fact enter it, for they will generally be seen to fall into these aridities."[43] And he feels, as do the others, that it is an indispensable stage in spiritual growth. "For the night belongs to the sensual part of the soul, and through it, the soul must pass in order to attain union with God."[44] After the individual has passed through these first two stages of spiritual development, there follows an intermediate interval of relative quiet, the purpose of which is to prepare the soul for the greater dark night of the soul which corresponds to "the great desolation." This in turn is followed by the last two stages, the illuminative and unitive, which can broadly be described as full spiritual maturity.

But it is the dark night of the senses that is of primary concern here. John of the Cross describes it largely in the terms already presented, as "the privation of every kind of pleasure which belongs to desire,"[45] and remarks in general that "... the soul finds no pleasure or consolation in the things of God, nor in any created thing."[46] In addition, he notes the ambivalence that is common to depressives of all kinds. The fear of God and the desire to please Him increases in this arid night. And John of the Cross also comments on the withdrawal that usually follows the grief reaction: "together with the aridity and the emptiness which it causes in the senses, it gives the soul an inclination and desire to be alone and in quietness, without being able to think of any particular thing or having the desire to do so."[47] Thus, the overall symptomatic picture presented in desolation is one of a person who is overwhelmed with the feeling of loss, is sad, self-depreciative, finding no satisfaction in himself or his environment, is physically inert, anxious, suffering from anorexia, insomnia, unable to pray or to love. As in the case of the neurotic depressive reaction, there is no accompanying misinterpretation of the outside world, although there is a lowering of intellectual activity.

Dynamics

On the other hand, one does not find in the literature on desolation the same dynamic factors that are present in the etiology of depression. There is no mention of either the constitutional predisposition or those psychogenic factors generally underlying the neurotic depressive reaction. Rather, the dynamics are described in terms of two factors: the external action of God, and the internal attitudes of response. The etiology is generally described in terms of ". . . a directly desolating action of God."[48] This action is purgative in quality. In a sense, God strips the person of natural pleasures in order that he may then fasten more exclusively on God alone. John of the Cross describes this process repeatedly. "The cause of this aridity is that God transfers to the spirit the good things, and the strength of the senses, which, since the soul's natural strength and senses are incapable of using them, remain barren, dry and empty."[49] The purpose of the action is preparatory and leads to a kind of purification. In this purification which results from the weaning of the person from natural desires there is a loss of all created things and a temporary feeling of the loss of God Himself. Again, John of the Cross describes this divine purpose:

> First, the soul must cast away all strange gods—namely all strange affections; secondly, it must purify itself of the remnants which the desires aforementioned have left in the soul, by means of the dark night of the senses whereof we are speaking, habitually denying them . . . so that God may change the soul, that its operations, which before were human, might become Divine.[50]

The internal response of the individual to this purgative aridity is the sense of loss, the grief, the dryness, which is regulated by the feeling that one is not serving God as he should.

> The purgative aridity is ordinarily accompanied by solicitude, with care and grief, as I say, because the soul is not serving God . . . and this feeling of grief produces a purgative

effect upon the desire, since the desire is deprived of all pleasure, and has its care centered upon God.[51]

This conviction that one is not serving God adequately, and therefore is deserving of His disdain, is fostered by God, precisely "... in order to lead them in the way of the spirit."[52]

This cursory review of the two phenomena of the neurotic depressive reaction and spiritual desolation bears out the observation that although the vocabulary often differs, the symptomatology of both is very much alike. In both states, the person suffers physically from anorexia, insomnia, general inertia and weakness. He is sad, indifferent, lonely and withdrawn. There is an impairment of intellectual acuity and an overwhelming feeling of self-depreciation. And in both instances, the reaction is characterized by a sense of loss. But the dynamics appear to be altogether different. The spiritual desolation is primarily of divine origin and serves the purpose of a purgative preparation, stripping the individual of sensible consolation so that he may progress to higher stages of union with God. On the other hand, the predominant theme that runs through the literature on the dynamics of the neurotic depressive reaction is the degree of self-preoccupation, self-centeredness and masochistic concern resulting from the loss of a loved object. It is, therefore, hypothesized that though the neurotic depressive reaction and spiritual desolation are symptomatically alike, they are dynamically distinct and can be distinguished on the grounds of the presence of narcissism.

Narcissism

The word "narcissism" was first used in a clinical sense by Havelock Ellis, and then by Nacke from whom Freud, as he himself states,[53] borrowed the term. For Ellis and Nacke, it denoted the perverse attitude of a person who treats his own body as if it were a sexual object. The word is derived etymologically from the Greek "narke," from which root we also have the words "narcosis," "narcotics," etc. But the Freudian analysis is based on the famed Greek legend.

Narcissus was the handsome youth who rejected the love of the nymph Echo. As a result of his rejection, she died of a broken heart, and Narcissus was condemned by Nemesis, the goddess of retributive justice, to fall in love with his own reflection in a pond. Narcissus pined away in self-admiration, and at death, was changed into the flower which bears his name. This is, however, not the only account of the legend of Narcissus. In his study of the origin of the myth, von Wieseler relates four distinct stories.[54] The earliest dates from the Greek of the heroic age and is attributed to Probas. In this account, the details are the same as in the version popular today except for the fact that Narcissus did not pine away in self-admiration. He was killed by a rejected suitor. Homosexuality, as we know from the legends of the court of the poetess Sappho, was not uncommon at this period. The second account is traced to another Greek poet of a later period, Conon. In this variation, Narcissus kills himself. A third myth, attributed to Pausanias, is still different. In it, Echo is actually Narcissus' twin sister, his duplicate in every possible way, and he loves her. She dies, however, and Narcissus tries to recapture her image by gazing at his own reflection. His death in this case is the result of intense mourning. The legend, in the form we now have it, dates to the Latin poet Ovid. There is a part of the legend, however, that is not generally heeded. The story actually begins with the account of how the river god, Cephisus, ravishes Liriope in his waters. From this aquatic union, Narcissus is born. Perhaps one could say that it was his mother that Narcissus saw in the water of the pond.

Actually, von Wieseler believes that the whole myth is a concoction to explain the origin of the flower, the Narcissus. The similarities are striking: the flower has an affinity for water, and always grows on the banks of streams or near water; it is slender of stem, and usually is found bending over toward the water; it usually has an asexual botanical reproduction; it is a very lovely plant; and it is highly poisonous. From all these varied forms of the legend, different analytical interpretations have arisen. The important thing is that, in all cases, Narcissus died because of the self-destruction wrought by self-love. And, indeed, in the development of the concept of narcissism since Freud, narcissistic self-love has come to mean a form of self-destruction.

It was Freud who gave the term the psychiatric popularity it now enjoys, although it did not appear in his writings until 1914. At that juncture, it marked a significant change in his career and necessitated a revision of his instinctual theory. Freud first used the word in a lecture given to the Vienna psychoanalytic Society in 1909, and then devoted an essay to it in 1914.[55] He used the conception of narcissism on evidence drawn from many sources, but the main impetus, as he himself says, came from Karl Abraham, who, as early as 1908, had pointed out that the main characteristic of dementia praecox was that the investment of objects with libido (sexual drive) was lacking. Abraham had also conjectured that the libido in such patients had been turned back upon the ego. From those reflections, Freud concluded that the libido, normally attached to objects, can abandon the objects and set the ego itself in their place. He also thought that such a narcissism was the universal, primal condition out of which later object love develops.

The clinical data upon which Freud based his concept of narcissism were as follows: the paraphrenic manifestations of megalomania, together with a magical belief in the "omnipotence of thoughts," to be found in dementia praecox; the self-absorption that takes place in sleep; the withdrawal of love and interest from the outside world in cases of painful illness; the body-attention of the hypochondriac; the self-preoccupation of old age; and forms of passionate love.[56] Of the last, Freud commented on the two ways in which one chose the love object: the anaclitic object choice, in which the choice fell upon a mother-substitute (for a male) and a protector (for a female), and the narcissistic object choice, in which the object corresponds to the picture one has of one-self.

Freud proceeded to make a number of basic distinctions. He first distinguished narcissism from egoism, on the grounds that when one speaks of egoism there is reference to the interests of the person concerned, whereas narcissism relates only to the satisfaction of needs. In addition, he distinguished narcissism from autoeroticism, since narcissism could be expressed in fantasy alone, without accompanying sex gratification. Of greatest importance is his distinction between primary and secondary narcissism. Applied to the child, narcissism meant for Freud the normal stage of early development. This was a primary narcissism, a universal, original condition of self-love, a primarily physiological condition out of which later object love develops. Secondary narcissism applied to those pathological states in which object-cathexis was, for varying reasons, withdrawn, and redirected to the ego. Many authors object to the application of the term "narcissism" to the infant's condition; for there is at that stage no question of a "withdrawal" of cathexis. Whatever the validity of the term "primary narcissism," it suffices to say that the pathological condition about which Freud wrote is properly called secondary narcissism. It is in this sense that we use the word in this study.

After 1914, the subject of narcissism occupied much of Freud's writings and tended to shape a good deal of his thought. It was the inspiration for his dual instinct theories. Heinz Hartman summarizes the contribution of the theory of narcissism in Freud's later work by saying that "... it marked the development of 'ego' psychology, but ran the greater danger of treating the ego as if it were the id."[57] Whatever the effects on Freud's psychology, the term remains with us. Brenner comments that it remains "... a useful and necessary working hypothesis in psychoanalytic theory, involving in a general way the hypercathexis of the self, the hypocathexis of the environment, and a pathologically immature relationship to these objects."[58]

Jung and Adler refrained from using the term "narcissism," possibly because Freud's original paper in 1914 was intended as a polemic addressed primarily to them. Jung, in brief, saw narcissism as a re-creation of the mother-child relationship, in which the individual, retreating before his own problems, dips for a moment into the source of life in order to wrest a little more strength from the mother. Adler's emphasis on the social sense and community commitment in the development of a mature style of life would imply that he, too, viewed narcissism as a pathological attitude. For him, it was the fictional creation of the super person in response to a radically felt inadequacy. Karen Horney later stated that narcissism "... means that the person loves and admires himself for values for which there is no adequate foundation ... in order to escape an unbearable feeling of nothingness."[59] This is more accurately described as self-inflation, a substitute for the genuine sense of self of which the person is deprived.

Freud and his immediate disciples regarded narcissism as a tendency toward artificial self-aggrandizement; but Menninger, Fromm, Weiss, Hartmann and most authors of today made a radical switch in emphasis. As the original legend itself strongly suggests, self-aggrandizement is not the only element, indeed, perhaps not the most significant one. Such an unrealistic self-love is radically a self-destructive force. Consequently, most contemporary authors prefer to think of the narcissistic ego cathexis as self-destructive rather than self-enhancing. Hartmann argues that, if narcissism is to be regarded as the cathexis of the ego with libidinal energies, and if such a cathexis is to be extended in the personality structure to include aggressive energies, the intimate relationship of self-love and self-punishment becomes apparent. Erich Fromm virtually reverses the original Freudian interpretation so that it becomes an inverted form of self-hate. He writes:

> The person incapable of love for others is in actual fact incapable of loving himself also. All his meticulous attention to

his body, his conceit, his general self-centeredness are not evidence of love of self, but are attempts to hide the feelings of failure and unlovability.[60]

In another passage, Fromm remarks that Freud's theory was consistent with the cultural standard of the times.

> The teachings of Luther and Calvin emphasize salvation only through the loss of self and the belittling of self. Any concern for the self was considered selfishness and was incompatible with love for others. It is possible that this cultural attitude kept Freud from seeing that narcissism as clinically observed is not self-love but self-hate.

Karl Menninger repeatedly emphasizes this new perception of the narcissistic syndrome in his analysis of the masochistic, self-destructive urge. He writes:

> ... the life instinct can find satisfaction, paradoxically in self-inflicted death ... it depends on that deadliest of erotic investments, narcissism. To kill oneself instead of being executed or slain is to retain for oneself the illusion of being omnipotent, since one is even by and in the act of suicide, master of life and death. Such omnipotence fantasies ... are to be regarded as infantile relics.[62]

In another place, with equal strength:

> The effects of such a narcissism are stultifying and deadening. Nothing inhibits love so much as self-love and from no source can we expect greater ameliorative results than from the deflection of this love from a self-investment to its proper investment in outside objects. ... Narcissism chokes and smothers the ego it hopes to protect.[63]

And again:

> ... instead of ameliorating contacts with the outside world, the libido entirely devoted to the nurture and protection of the ego remains inert, a coagulated lump of narcissism.[64]

This same theme is stressed by Eidelberg in a series of articles on the concept of narcissistic mortification.[65] This he defines as the experience by the total personality of a sudden loss of control over internal or external reality, or both. It is related to the child's reaction to the first mortification, the experience that it is not omnipotent in its helplessness. There are two such mortifications: the first, internal, occurs when the child realizes the limitations of its power over itself; and the second, external, when the child realizes the limitations of its power over the external world. Such mortifications are essential for ego development, but they can be repressed or denied. If they are, a sustained feeling of power can result. When this artificial sense of power later confronts an unyielding environment the inadequacy stands in conflict with the power, and the combination of feelings of omnipotence with experienced inadequacy creates a narcissistic depression. The individual, he says, needs to think himself responsible, i.e., to have power over another, and failures in such power create the continued shock that there is such a lack of power. In order to defend against the loss of power, the individual must provoke rejections by another, in order that he may still feel some power even for bad. Such a feeling of power, coupled with inadequacy and guilt, turns the ego punitively upon itself, and the masochistic elements of a reactive depression are manifest.

In summary, narcissism can be defined as the withdrawal of cathexis from objects in favor of a libidinal concentration on the ego or ego functions. This implies the creation of an artificial ego constructed by the individual to compensate in some way for the feeling of personal inadequacy. As such, it can have two distinct faces. It may appear clinically as self-aggrandizement, megalomania, omnipotence, magical thinking, self-admiration. Or it may appear in some form of self-destruction, masochism, desperate need for attention, self-punishment.

Narcissism and the Neurotic Depressive Reaction

Among the early psychoanalysts, Abraham and Fenichel noted repeatedly the narcissistic content of depression. Abraham felt that in the melancholia there was a withdrawal of cathexis from the outside world as a result of the painful experience of the loss of the loved object, and the subsequent reinvestment of that cathexis on the ego. Fenichel noted that predisposition to depressive reaction is present in people who require a great deal of narcissistic gratification. Allers, writing in 1937 of the difference between the two kinds of "aridité," described the neurotic depressive in similar terms: "In neurosis, there is an obsession with the self, and an incapacity to give oneself, so much so, that one can doubt whether such a deformed soul is able to arrive at the degree of interior life requisite of dynamic aridity."[66] And Jaeger in 1955 wrote that in the reactive depressive, one found "... the personality components of excessive narcissistic cathexis of the ego." And he concluded the same article with the observation that:

> Some individuals show so much self-centered libido, so much preoccupation with their own person that they are unable to give love; they depend on the love they receive from the outside world, not on real achievement. A threat to their narcissistic supply is intolerable to them, and is as a rule, met with bitterness and resentment ... and results in a depressive reaction.[67]

Gutheil, in the *American Handbook of Psychiatry,* noted that "... the reactive depressive is deprived of narcissistic supplies," and the neurotic depressive reaction is "... a narcissistic injury." And Arieti, in an address to the American Psychiatric Association, linked the depressive reaction to conflicts growing in an inner-directed culture.

Despite the degree to which narcissism has been linked with the depressive reaction in theoretical literature, there have been few reported attempts to verify the hypothesis experimentally, if that can be done. It would be precisely in a research of this nature that the psychologist of religion or the pastoral counselor might focus his special interdisciplinary interest. For there is the strong suggestion that stages of ascetical desolation, as described in the work of so many spiritual writers, and phases of neurotic depression can be distinguished on the basis of the presence or absence of dynamic narcissism, despite the fact that the two phenomena can appear to be symptomatically the same.

Much, as has already been noted, has been written recently in the field of pastoral or religious psychology. There has been little, however, in the way of genuine synthesis. Focusing on very specific problems that require considerable interdisciplinary expertise and experience and bringing the wisdom of both disciplines to bear on that specific area may accomplish what the massive overviews have hitherto failed to do. It is to this end that the diagnosis of differences between depression and desolation is here offered as a sample case for pastoral psychology.

Notes

1. M. Lot-Borodine, "L'Aridité ou Siccitas dans l'Antiquité Chrétienne," in *Etudes Carmelitaines,* 22nd Yr., Vol. 2 (Oct., 1937), p. 194.
2. *Ibid.,* p. 195.
3. Alphonsus Rodriguez, *The Practice of Perfection and Christian Virtues,* 3 vols., American ed., trans, Joseph Rickaby, S.J. (Chicago: Loyola University Press, 1929), Vol. 2, pp. 481-482.
4. Charles Grimbert, "L'Aridité et Certaines Processus Psychopathiques," in *Etudes Carmelitaines,* 22nd year, Vol. 2 (Oct., 1937), p. 121.
5. Rudolph Allers, "Aridité Symptome et Aridité Stade," in *Etudes Carmelitaines, op. cit.,* p. 132.
6. Grimbert, *op. cit.,* p. 121.
7. Rodriguez, *op. cit.,* p. 484.
8. Allers, *op. cit.,* p. 132.
9. Edward Stainbrook, "A Cross-cultural Evaluation of Depressive Reac-

tions," in *Depression,* eds. Paul H. Hoch and Joseph Zubin (New York: Grune & Stratton, Inc., 1954), p. 43.

10. *Ibid.,* p. 45.

11. Edward Ascher, "A Criticism of the Concept of Neurotic Depression," in the *American Journal of Psychiatry,* Vol. 108 (1952), p. 901.

12. *Ibid.,* p. 904.

13. R. A. Cleghorn and G. C. Curtis, "Depression, Mood, Symptom, Syndrome," in *Documenta Geigy: Acta Psychosomatica,* No. 2, North American Series (September, 1959), pp. 18-19.

14. Jacob Jaeger, "Mechanisms in Depression," in *American Journal of Psychiatry* (1955), Vol. 9, p. 441.

15. Emil Gutheil, "Reactive Depressions," in *American Handbook of Psychiatry* (New York: Basic Books, Inc., 1959), p. 345.

16. Cleghorn and Curtis, *op. cit.,* p. 15.

17. Sigmund Freud, "Mourning and Melancholia," in *A General Selection from the Works of Sigmund Freud,* ed. John Rickman (New York: Doubleday & Co., 1957), pp. 124-140.

18. Cleghorn and Curtis, *op. cit.,* pp. 30-35.

19. Paul Keilholz, "Diagnosis and Therapy of the Depressive States," in *Documenta Geigy, op. cit.,* (August, 1959), p. 20ff.

20. Freud, *op. cit.,* pp. 127-135.

21. Karl Abraham, "Manic-Depressive States and the Pregenital Levels of the Libido," in *Selected Papers on Psychoanalysis* (New York: Basic Books, Inc., 1942), p. 453.

22. Melanie Klein, *The Psycho-analysis of Children* (London: Hogarth Press, 1932), p. 38ff.

23. E. Jacobsen, "The Self and the Object World: Vicissitudes of Their Infantile Cathexes and Their Influence on Ideational and Affective Development," in *The Psychoanalytic Study of the Child* (New York: International Universities Press, 1954), Vol. 9, pp. 75-127.

24. Norman Cameron, *Personality Development and Psychopathology* (Boston: Houghton Mifflin Co., 1963), pp. 516-557.

25. *Cf.* Irenee Hausheer, "Penthos," in *Orientalia Christiana Analecta* (Rome: Pontifical Institute of Oriental Studies, 1944), Vol. 132, p. 26.

26. *Ibid.,* p. 27.

27. *Ibid.,* p. 8.

28. Henri Martin, "Desolation," in *Dictionnaire de la Spiritualité Ascétique et Mystique* (Paris: Beauchesne, 1957), Vol. 3, p. 640.

29. Rodriguez, *op. cit.,* Vol. 2, p. 459.

30. Justin McCann, ed. *The Cloud of Unknowing* (Westminster, Md.: Newman Press, 1952), 6th ed., p. 78ff.

31. Louis Chardon, *La Croix de Jesus* (Paris: Bertier, 1647; Editions du Cerf, 1937).

32. Augustine Baker, *The Great Desolation* (London: A. Devine, 1876), pp. 536-541.

33. Bruno de Jesus-Marie, "Saint Jean de la Croix et la Psychologie Moderne," in *Etudes Carmelitaines,* 30th Year, Vol. 2 (May, 1951), pp. 9-24.

34. Martin, *op. cit.,* p. 640, and Daeschler, "Aridité," in *Dictionnaire, op. cit.,* Vol. 1, pp. 843-855.

35. Daeschler, *op. cit.,* p. 843.

36. Louis de la Trinite, "Sèche et Obscure Nuit de Contemplation," in *Etudes Carmelitaines,* 22nd year, Vol. 2 (Oct., 1937), p. 208.

37. Martin, "Dereliction," in *Dictionnaire, op. cit.,* Vol. 3, p. 505.

38. *Cf.,* Martin, "Desolation," pp. 641ff.

39. *Ibid.,* p. 633.

40. Ignatius of Loyola, *Exercitia Spiritualia* (Rome: Typis Polyglotis Vaticanis, 1948), p. 223.

41. John of the Cross, *Ascent of Mount Carmel* (New York: Doubleday & Co., 1958).

42. John of the Cross, *Dark Night of the Soul* (New York: Doubleday & Co., 1959).

43. *Ibid.,* p. 63.

44. John of the Cross, *Ascent of Mount Carmel,* pp. 26-27.

45. *Ibid.,* p. 24.

46. John of the Cross, *Dark Night of the Soul, op. cit., p. 64.*

47. *Ibid.,* p. 66.

48. Martin, *op. cit.,* p. 640.

49. John of the Cross, *Dark Night of the Soul, op. cit.* p. 65.

50. ———, *Ascent of Mount Carmel, op. cit.,* p. 37.

51. ———, *Dark Night of the Soul, op. cit.,* p. 65.

52. *Ibid.,* p. 68.

53. Sigmund Freud, "The Theory of the Libido: Narcissism," in *A General Introduction to Psychoanalysis* (New York: Liveright Pub. Corp., 1943), p. 357.

54. Baron von Wieseler, *Narkissos* (Gottingen: Dietrich, 1856).

55. Sigmund Freud, "On Narcissism: An Introduction," in *A General Selection from the Works of Sigmund Freud, op. cit.,* pp. 104-123.

56. *Ibid.,* pp. 112ff.

57. Heinz Hartmann, "The Mutual Influences in the Development of the Ego and the Id," in *The Psychoanalytic Study of the Child, op. cit.* (1952), Vol. 7, p. 17.

58. Charles Brenner, *An Elementary Textbook of Psychoanalysis* (New York: Doubleday and Co., 1957), p. 110.

59. Horney, *op. cit.,* p. 194.

60. Clara Thompson, *Psychoanalysis: Evolution and Development* (New York: Hermitage Press, 1950), p. 69.

61. Erich Fromm, *Man for Himself* (New York: Rinehart & Co., Inc., 1947), p. 139.
62. Karl Menninger, *Man Against Himself* (New York: Harcourt, Brace and World, Inc., 1938), p. 63.
63. *Ibid.,* p. 381.
64. *Ibid.,* p. 382.
65. Ludwig Eidelberg, "Introduction to the Study of Narcissistic Mortification," in *Psychiatric Quarterly,* Vol. 31 (1957), pp. 658-688; Vol. 33 (1959), pp. 636-646.
66. Rudolph Allers, "Aridité Symptome et Aridité Stade," *op. cit.,* p. 194.
67. Jacob Jaeger, "Mechanisms of Depression," in *American Journal of Psychotherapy,* Vol. 9 (1955), p. 451.
68. Emil Gutheil, "Reactive Depression," *op. cit.,* p. 349.

7. Student Counseling: The Transaction

An historian of some note once defined history as "... a case of just one damn thing after another." This definition seems not so facetious when applied to the history of the student counseling movement. For it is a strange history. Counseling, at once both young and old, is a bit like a tiny infant, whose wrinkled face bears the lines of old age. Sir Winston Churchill once overheard a woman remark of a nearby infant, "Why, that baby looks just like Sir Winston." Churchill retorted characteristically, "Madam, all babies look like me." It is much this way with that human encounter that we have come to call counseling; for in the long history of man's attempts to understand and to assist other men, counseling, as a specific technique for achieving that end, is only forty years of age.

Because of its youth, we cannot expect too much of it. It is often helpless as an infant, in need of the watchful hand of its parent disciplines, often restless to be its own master, but never quite knowing how best to go about it. Because of its youth, it must leave many problems unanswered. Indeed, because of its youth, we cannot even formulate a definition acceptable to all of what counseling is all about.

And yet, though young, the art of counseling is centuries old. Modern counseling techniques, like modern psychology, did not arise on the scene of man's history like Venus on a seashell. The knowledgeable counselor cannot help but hear in his own words echoes of Sophocles and the chorus of the Greek tragedies. He cannot help but hear Aretaeus of Rome who, 17 centuries before the categories of Kraepelin in 1899, gave a description and mode of treatment for melancholia that rivals much that is modern. It is patent that in our understanding of man we have not come very far. So the great experimentalist, Ebbinghaus, noted that "psychology has a long past, but a short history."[1]

There is another problem in the history of counseling. Even psychology, its immediate parent, itself both young and old, is a hybrid offspring. Psychology has never really been its own master. It has had to content itself with living in the shadow of the traditional disciplines of philosophy and the physical sciences. From the Golden Age of the Greeks until the middle of the nineteenth century, psychology was the handmaid of Philosophy. Aristotle's *De Anima,*[2] for example, though not without a certain measure of scientific observation, is basically philosophical in method. It structures empirical data according to a metaphysical model. So also is the work of Aquinas, Descartes, Kant and all the psychologists of the post-Renaissance period.

Historians suggest that psychology came of age in the nineteenth century when she was caught up in that optimistic and surging tide of the new scientific method. Wilhelm Wundt and, on this continent, William James, brought man, or at least parts of him, into the same laboratory where the rest of nature was being carefully dissected. The Weber-Fechner law became a symbol of the new movement, presumed proof that human behavior could also be measured along a physical scale. But it appears that this emancipation from philosophy brought with it no great autonomy for psychology. Sheltered for centuries, it merely exchanged parents to become the handmaid of physics. And now again, there are signs that psychology is once again in search of a parent. Perhaps we are witnessing today psychology's adolescence, and perhaps it will find its own identity shortly; but as yet, we are in no position to say. In any event, with such a dubious lineage, we cannot expect counseling to exhibit the characteristics of full maturity.

If that were not enough, counseling has, quite apart from psychology, a few ancestors of its own. In North America it grew out of the field of education, in Germany out of vocational placement, and in France out of psychotherapy. We can place the beginning of the new movement in North America at about 1910, with the introduction of the first guidance programs. At that point counseling was totally the property of the school. And, of course, within such a framework, the counselor served as a teacher of sorts. His function was didactic; he was an adviser, a surrogate parent. He diagnosed the problem, imparted information, lectured a bit, encouraged and proposed solutions.

Then around 1942, the world of counseling was turned upside down. The nondirective, "client-centered" approach of Carl Rogers[3] is literally the inverse of pre-Rogerian counseling. Without dealing at length with the psychological background for "client-centered" counseling, the basic hypotheses about the person upon which Rogers builds are these: every individual has within himself the resources to solve his own problems; every individual has perfect freedom of decision; the main drives and conflicts to be resolved in counseling are emotional; and the present is more important than the past.

With these canons established, it becomes apparent that the active role in counseling is now the counselee's; for he alone knows his own inner world, not the counselor who serves rather as a catalyst to assist him to utilize his own resources in an atmosphere of absolute freedom. For Rogers, there is no diagnosis, no prognosis. Counseling is no longer focused upon a problem, as some mental cryptogram, but on the person. And since the inner world is more emotional than intellectual, new techniques are to be employed: the acceptance of the client in a permissive atmosphere, and the reflection of his contemporary feeling tone. These characteristics of permissiveness, acceptance, reflection, and so on, are responsible for those abundant caricatures of the nondirective therapist, with which all are familiar.

Whatever the objections, Rogers remained uncontested king for a number of years. He had taken the pains to support his claims with experimental evidence. For lack of contrary evidence, no one could really say how valid his experiments were. But with characteristic American respect for experimental evidence, the opposition was temporarily silenced. In time, however, contrary evidence was forthcoming. Eysenck[4] and many others ran experiments which appeared to indicate that there were about 60 per cent cures no matter what type of therapy, directive or nondirective, was used. The data appeared to say that something other than the specific technique was involved.

This action-reaction pattern is quite characteristic of the whole history of psychology. Pre-Rogerian counseling stressed the intellectual aspects of the student's problem; the Rogerian revolt placed the emphasis squarely on the emotional. In the atmosphere of battle that followed, an "either-or" situation was created. One camp suggested that, if you think, you must not be able to feel, and could not counsel. The extreme produced a kind of emotional anarchy and a Mary Worth approach to counseling. The other held to the dogma that feeling would obstruct proper rational control, and a sort of cold, dispassionate, academic relationship resulted. It is time to put the counselor back together again, to let him be a complete feeling, thinking animal, to let him encounter not just a gerrymandered client, not just parts of people, not just a person who feels, or a person who thinks, but *both*.

From this history, we know at least something about what counseling is not. Above all it is not a relationship which nourishes the dependence of the client upon the counselor. Such dependence is immeasurably harmful. It is perhaps an especial threat when the counselor appears to need the client as much, if not more, than the client needs him. The goal of counseling is never dependence in itself, although for a period, as in the transference in Freudian analysis, it may be necessary. But, as in all forms of education, the goal is separation, of child from parent, of student from professor, of client from counselor. The goal is reached when the client can honestly and simply say to the counselor, "I no longer need you." Though this declaration, for reasons of our own countertransference, can cause us a twinge of regret, it is in fact the supreme tribute to the counselor. He above all must respect the integrity of the person whom he is encountering and must always work for his growth and his independence.

That could serve, in fact, as a definition of counseling—a unique, professional, purposeful and human encounter between two persons in which the presence of the one with his training, skill and personality awakens the genuine potential of the other, who by that means can come to relate more productively to himself and to his neighbor. In this definition I mean to exclude those forms of psychotherapy which are concerned with people who, because of the gravity of their disturbance, are unable to respond to milder forms. I mean as well to exclude the enormous variety of genuinely therapeutic "bull-sessions" which, though immensely beneficial in their own right, do not presume to be conscious, professional counseling. Many of the arts of counseling, as practiced by bartenders, cab drivers, beauticians and busboys, may be enormously successful; but for the moment, we must restrict ourselves to those whose precise purpose is to counsel and who do it within the canons of some contemporary theory.

Lewis Wolberg[5] has done an admirable job of restricting the field. He first distinguishes supportive therapy, which includes guidance work, drug therapy, forms of catharsis, etc., from insight therapy. And the latter, he subdivides into reeducative, insofar as its concern is conscious readjustment of attitudes, and reconstructive, where the focus is largely on the unconscious. As counselors, especially in the school and church setting, we are concerned with supportive therapy by way of the sharing of guidance information of all kinds, by acceptance, encouragement and catharsis and with reeducative insight by whichever of the contemporary techniques we may feel inclined to choose.

Requisites

Regardless of which theoretical persuasion we do prefer, we are all concerned with what goes on before, during and after the counseling interviews themselves, and much of that does not differ from school to school. Otto Fenichel provides a short list of indications requisite for any counseling.[6] First, we must attend to the age, intelligence and life situation of the client. For those in the schools these are no real problems. Students all fall within the range of those considered most amenable to counseling. We must then, he says, be concerned with the severity of the problem. In this respect, I think we should feel no regrets in recognizing our own limitations. The magical thinking that we can somehow cure all is singularly dangerous. When the client's malaise is severe, he should obviously be referred to whatever psychiatrist hopefully is associated in some way with the school or parish. Signs of such disturbance are not difficult to detect. Marked dissociations in speech and thought patterns, gross symptomatic conversation states, such as skin rashes and nervous tremors, manifest paranoid feelings, delusions and hallucinations, a depression that renders the client virtually inert, these and many others are signals that professional attention is immediately necessary and should be summoned. Fenichel adds that the character structure of the client should be such as to make prognosis promising, and here psychological testing may be of help in assessing the necessary strength of the ego. It is well also to consider, before counseling, the vigor of the secondary gains, those defense mechanisms which the client has been employing to protect himself. How deep are his rationalizations, his compensations, his compulsive rituals, and how necessary are they to him? Can we provide something that is more satisfactory to him than those defenses which he has felt himself obliged to build?

At the outset, we are well-advised to take note immediately of the attitudes of the client and, indeed, of our own attitudes. How does he feel toward this situation? If he is aggressive, and many will be, what is my countertransference? Can I absorb his hostility and repeatedly? In some way, he will surely test to see if, despite his provocative behavior, we are still prepared to accept him. Perhaps he is inclined to feel that for some reason he should be rejected because he always has been, and he will expect this rejection as confirmation of his own long-standing feelings. Should we oblige him, and we may be sorely tempted to do so, his behavior patterns will merely be reinforced. The time and place for the counseling interview are also factors to be considered. They need not, however, concern us overly much. Everyone is sufficiently aware of the need for private, reasonable office space; and most are just as aware of the difficulty of persuading administrations and superiors of that need.

The Transaction

After considering indications and counterindications for counseling, we can turn our attention to the dynamics functioning within the process itself. In doing so, we immediately confront two oft-repeated and "magical" words: rapport and insight. Of the first, I do not wish to say much, because lengthy discussions tend to make it awfully artificial. We are prone to reify rapport, to make it a "thing." As we have seen, there are no ingredients one can mix according to a recipe to "make rapport." It is, nonetheless, a *sine qua non.*

The second magic word is "insight," and it, too, has been abused. We often call insight that for which we have no evidence. But far from this, true insight is built solidly on evidence, however acquired, by testing, by observation, by the self-revelation of the client himself. It presumes that information has been gathered by some means and that some diagnosis has been made, be it expressed or unexpressed. Because of their awareness of the danger of labels in this respect, contemporary counselors prefer to express diagnosis, if it is to be expressed at all, in descriptive terms. They attempt to capture the individual himself and not just a classification.

There is, of course, insight on the part of the client, too. He develops a keener understanding of himself and an increased degree of emotional self-acceptance. All of the problems we face as counselors can somehow be reduced to an improper mode of self-acceptance, or the total lack of it. The creation, therefore, of an atmosphere in which the client can accept himself is a prime dynamic function of the counselor. In it, the client comes to accept and face those facts or feelings which he has hitherto carefully hidden from view. And as he gains in self-knowledge and self-acceptance, so does the counselor.

There is a rather crucial point in the early stages of every counseling relationship which must be maneuvered successfully, I think, if such self-acceptance is to come. In order to accept himself, the client must experience genuine acceptance by another, in this instance, the counselor. And he will quickly test that acceptance by feeling out the counselor. Perhaps he will begin to describe in broad terms how he feels, suspecting that the counselor, as all before him, will not quite understand. He is asking quite clearly: "Do you understand me?" "Do you accept me?" The counselor must be ready for this moment. He must recognize it, and immediately enter into the client's own frame of reference, and there redescribe for him in a mode he can understand *just how he feels.* The moment is a trifle like getting through the breakers and into open sea. If one manages well, there is smooth sailing ahead; if not, there is real danger of capsizing then and there.

There are, of course, other dynamic factors at play within the sessions themselves including the comments that the counselor chooses to make. He can either reflect the present level of the client's progress and attendant feeling tone, or he can focus on some remarks that merit highlighting, or he can confront the client with some nuance of which the client is but dimly aware. Whatever the level of the comment, it ought to be purposeful, built upon what the client himself says and feels, and timely. There is precious little gain in commenting or interpreting beyond the readiness of the client to understand. And it can be agonizing for the counselor to know what insight the client should be sharing with him, and not be able to say it because the client is simply not ready to hear it. In the process of counseling, patients learn patience with themselves; so do counselors.

Whether or not there is to be some planning during the interviews depends largely on the purpose of the interviews. If they are vocational or specifically educational, there is need for testing of abilities and aptitudes, interpretation of data for the client and assistance in making an appropriate choice. This is a pretty straightforward operation, but it does require a breadth of information, an important part of the counselor's repertoire. At times it may be his biggest service. In many areas, notably rural ones, the fear that can rise from ignorance is a considerable source of anxiety for the client. He can be immeasurably helped by information that the counselor can supply from a full, up-to-date library of resources.

In psychological counseling, as such, the function of planning is rather a moot point. For Rogers, planning, an intrusion on the client's freedom, is a *bête noir.* Many do feel, however, that a coordinated effort of combined stresses is desirable, and that, therefore, there should be some homework. By way of a concession to the nondirective schools, we might suggest that it is generally better to shift the responsibility for the plan and execution to the client himself, attending as always to his growth and independence.

Ending the Counseling Relationship

Ending the counseling relationship is a tender issue at times. Ideally, the interviews should be terminated when their purpose is attained, but that is not often clear. The purpose is a measure of maturity, or a "cure," if one can legitimately use that word. But there is no "cure" in counseling, in the medical sense, and the concept of maturity is one that bristles with problems. Normally, we would conclude the interviews at the mutual agreement of both persons, or when the presenting problem has been resolved, or when the client feels he no longer needs counseling. It can be facilitated at times by lengthening the intervals between interviews. But there is, as always, no rule of thumb. There is, however, one red flag to be flown. Often, because of his dependency needs, the client will feign a certain sharpening of his maladjustive symptoms, realizing, perhaps not consciously, that this is the only way to continue a relationship that has been satisfying to him. The only way to keep the counselor is to keep the symptoms, and to this possibility we should be alert.

The Presenting Problems

Finally, it seems almost trite to remark that basic to the counseling relationship and second in importance only to the persons involved, are the presenting problems. These are legion! And the entire legion can at one time or another march through the student counselor's office. Each of these problems is unique, and must be treated so, for each client is a unique person. His problem is ontologically different because it is his, even though you may have heard the identical tale the hour before and hundreds of hours before that. Yet, within that awesome variety of individuals, there are patterns which reoccur and frequently. These you recognize easily. We have space here to mention only a few.

A good majority of counseling problems begin in the cloak of an educational or vocational choice, but few, I think, end there. Lurking underneath the educational problem is usually a personal one which the student, quite understandably, is loathe to divulge at first. Without any undue witch-hunting or probing on the part of the counselor, it will usually appear. Among the more common patterns we confront as counselors in the schools, there are the over-achievers, students whose motivation exceeds their talent. The highly competitive atmosphere of modern education is a little overwhelming for them. Exam panic or possibly pressure from home to succeed can bring some to the point of near collapse, and many to the point where their anxiety makes it impossible for them to study productively. And then the "bennies" and "speed" appear. The vicious circle is a common one. The greater the anxiety, the less can be learned; the poorer the performance, the greater the anxiety, and so on. It is a commonplace in learning theory that the correlation of motivation and learning is not linear. Indeed, after a certain point, increased motivation decreases learning prowess. For this student there is an enormous need to ventilate, to release tension, to lower pressure. If his sights are too high, he can often be genuinely relieved and rendered more functional if he can acknowledge it and begin to pursue his own ambitions rather than his parents' vicarious ones. No less frequent are the "underachievers," whose performance belies their ability. Something is blocking performance, family problems or problems of social identification, and these must be explored and exposed if the blockage is to be removed.

There are also the "doom-makers," students with a gnawing sense of personal inadequacy, so great at times that it generates a need to provoke failure in the classroom or in the social arena. Then the failure itself can stand for them as Exhibit A in confirmation of the feeling that was already there. For some time I counseled a young girl with such a need to fail, both socially and academically. Quite attractive, if she had left nature relatively undisturbed, she was so filled with feelings of self-depreciation that she was basically convinced that it was her lot in life to fail, and she did a splendid job of proving it to herself. She wore a beatnik dress, with straight unkempt hair and enough white lipstick and heavy mascara to give her a distinct resemblance to a skull. If this were not enough to produce a certain amount of social awkwardness, she would, when on a rare date, do everything in her power to insult the boy she was with, precisely so that when he did not call her for a subsequent rendezvous, she would defend her deep and fearful sense of inadequacy by rationalizing that it was because she had been rather chippy with him. The same failure-provoking activity characterized her academic ventures, failing to write exams, excusing herself on the grounds that she had not studied, etc. Behind the blasé indifference was a very frightened girl.

Another trying group are the victims of Psychology I. A little learning is dangerous. especially in an area so treacherous and so complex. The Psychology I graduate can fancy himself a sophisticated diagnostician, ferreting out subtle defense mechanisms in himself and others. He is a danger to himself as well as others. I recall one boy repeating to me on the basis of what he had learned of Adlerian psychology, "Well, after all, what can you expect of me? I'm an only child." Whatever domestic predicament he may have had, it was as nothing compared to his desire to exploit it.

The counselor will also be confronted with the full range of sexual problems from early marriage to homosexual panic. Relative to the latter, I have chosen the words consciously. There is so much said today of homosexuality, so much misleading pseudodata that a young student who feels uncertain about his own identity begins to wonder about his social relationships. So great can become his fear of becoming a homosexual that the chances of it are outrageously enlarged. Fear is never more than a step away from fascination. In this context, fearful preoccupation can be the grounds for experimental pseudohomosexual activity. I do not mean to imply that there is no homosexuality on the campus, but only that it is never so widespread as its surrogate facsimiles.

The drug scene on campus is the problem which unfortunately has received greatest notoriety in recent years. The counselor here is caught in the swirl of social hysteria. Unsubstantiated anecdotal claims run wild in an atmosphere of little genuine experimental data. The absence of facts about the hallucinogenic drugs especially tolerates a polarizing of extreme claims of instant mysticism on the one hand and certain physiological catastrophe on the other. Neither of these claims has, of course, much validity. Caught in this situation, the counselor must attempt to introduce some objectivity into this careening world. This specific problem has been dealt with, of course, at great length in other places. Of the counselor's role, Keniston remarks sagely that ". . . those of us who are critical of student drug abuse must demonstrate to our students that there are better and more lasting ways to experience the fullness, the depth, the variety and the richness of life than that of ingesting psychoactive chemicals."[7]

The Legal Issue in Drug Use

Compounding the problem is the legal issue which the counselor must face. He, as well as the student, confronts a patchwork of impulse legislation, especially with regard to marijuana and in some instances to LSD, with which he can scarcely agree. The situation raises obvious ethical implications. How does one conduct oneself before a law with which he disagrees, and before student practice in conflict with the law? More will be said of that in the final chapter. Drug education conferences established in many parts of the country have assisted in the amelioration of this situation. Nonetheless, the counselor is still first obliged to acquaint the student with the nature of the law and the penalties involved should he violate it. In the vast majority of instances, of course, students are already familiar with the law and processes of law enforcement. With this caution aside, it is then within his domain to explore the student's motivation in drug usage, the possible psychological effects, the ingredients of the inner experience the student enjoys and the possibilities, if any, of awakening him to other natural, nonsynthetic means of attaining a similar expansion of consciousness. It is no mean task.

Regardless of the enormous range of problems which do confront the counselor and the awesome variety of persons who suffer them, to each encounter he must bring the same personal qualifications. It is, therefore, indispensable that the counselor *listen*. At the risk of belaboring the oft-repeated point, listening, no matter how frequently its importance is noted, is still rare. Some listen with their ears to be sure, but one must listen also with the eyes, with the whole person. It is then that listening becomes therapeutic in itself. It is in this way that the counselor becomes accessible to the student. It is his "being-there," his "presence-to" the other that awakens the being of the student, to use the tortuous jargon of the existentialists. The existential group has been accused of fostering a movement whose sole value has been to invent ever new and hyphenated ways of rendering the verb "to be." Whatever validity that facetious jibe may have, it is true that the existentialists have continually stressed the one element which is essential for the counselor, especially when he is working with an academic clientele. For each student, regardless of his presenting problem, is somehow not in-his-world. And it is the work of the counselor to witness to that real world for him and gradually induce him to realize his unique "being-in-the-world," his place.

Notes

1. *Cf.,* Franz Alexander and Sheldon Selesnick, *The History of Psychiatry* (New York: Harper and Row, 1966).
2. *Cf.,* E. G. Boring, *A History of Experimental Psychology* (New York: Appleton-Century-Crofts, 1950).
3. *Cf.,* Carl Rogers, *Client-centered Therapy* (Boston: Houghton Miffiin Co., 1951).
4. H. J. Eysenck, "The Effects of Psychotherapy," in *Handbook of Abnormal Psychology* (New York: Basic Books, Inc., 1961), pp. 697-725.
5. Lewis Wolberg, *The Technique of Psychotherapy* 2nd ed., two parts (New York: Grune and Stratton, Inc., 1967).
6. Otto Fenichel, *The Psychoanalytic Theory of Neuroses* (New York: W.W. Norton and Co., Inc., 1945).
7. Kenneth Keniston, "Drug Use and Student Values." Paper originally presented at National Association of Student Personnel Administrators' Drug Education Conference, Washington, D.C. (Nov., 1966).

8. *Negotiating the*
Generation Gap

The "generation gap" that allegedly divides the young from those past thirty-five has become one of the more tiresome phrases of our neo-jargon. Employed long beyond its descriptive value, the phrase could just as easily now refer to some previously uncharted gulch in the Sierras, not unlike the Pass in which the Donner party met their fate en route to California. The analogy, though forced, is not without some merit. For through "generation gap" blow some rather treacherous winds, winds of change that sweep long-established structures before them and chill the withered bodies of those who can neither flee nor fight. And the trails through the gap are littered with the wreckage left by many who have attempted to negotiate passage.

The gap exists, I believe, as a result of our collective inability to heed the early warning system, as sounded in

Edgar Friedenberg's book *The Vanishing Adolescent*,[1] published in 1959 and read and reviewed widely since. Despite Friedenberg's very clearly stated proposition that young people simply are not the same as they used to be, the adult world has clung rather tenaciously to two misconceptions. The first is that the "adolescent" is what he is supposed to be. And that has been determined with unequivocal and changeless clarity by textbooks on adolescent psychology. The second is that since most of us were required to endure high school and college in our youth, we can presume to know what these institutions are currently like. They are now as they were when we were in them, and the experiences one has in them must be essentially the same today as they were twenty years ago. I would contend that these common assumptions are not only invalid, but they are at the root of the misunderstanding and lack of communication that characterize the distance across the "generation gap."

The Myth of Adolescence

No country has studied the adolescent as thoroughly as the United States, and no country understands their adolescents as poorly. This long and exhaustive study was probably launched by G. Stanley Hall, the dean of American psychologists, first president of the American Psychological Association and the American who first invited Freud to the United States in 1909. Hall published in 1905 a two-volume set, *The Psychology of Adolescence,* which served as a base for subsequent studies.

Study piled upon study, building a mountain of myths which came to enjoy a measure of scientific credibility (or perhaps the illusion of scientific credibility) more as a result of internal consistency with what had already been written than as a result of empirical observation. Authors felt obliged to cite chapter and verse of the masterpiece, footnoting previous authors and drawing from earlier studies to create an atmosphere of scholarship and scientific authenticity. The "review of the literature," as any research scholar in the social sciences well knows, is an indispensable element in the reporting of research studies. Data about adolescence was dutifully passed from one author to another, with careful attention to the amenities of footnotes and bibliographies, but without much concern about the subjects themselves. As a result, one can scan almost any contemporary text on adolescence and discover to his astonishment that it differs in content only slightly from what G. Stanley Hall wrote in 1905. But while the textbook content was not changing, the young people certainly were. And to understand them in terms of Hall's careful description of 1905 is patently invalid.

In the main, this is the thrust of Friedenberg's well-advised title *The Vanishing Adolescent.* The concept "adolescence," if understood roughly in the sense in which most authors use it, is, according to Friedenberg, obsolete. The literature no longer enjoys empirical validity, for the breed described by Hall and others has simply vanished. The adolescent prototypes, Tom Brown at Oxford, Penrod, Huck Finn, Harold Teen, Henry Aldrich or whatever corresponds to one's vintage, have disappeared. And any attempt to understand the young of today in terms of these archetypes is bound to miss the target no matter how comfortable adults may feel with these concepts. The adolescent described in most texts and in popular *Reader's Digest* derivatives of the textbook material is simply as extinct as the dinosaur, an archaeological specimen to be found only in the archival tarpits of university libraries. Thinking about young people in such terms may have some value as an historical exercise to describe a species that once roamed the streets of our cities and the sands of our beaches, but it does not help us to understand the new generation much. Adolescence, as a distinct and fathomable stage of human development, like infancy, puberty, the menopause or senescence, is an obsolescent concept.

Premature Adulthood

Riesman accounts for this fact as follows:

> . . . traditional adolescence *is* vanishing, swallowed up at the
> childhood end by the increasing precocity of the young, their
> turning of high school into an ersatz college or even suburb,
> their early if somewhat flat maturity as lovers, consumers,
> committeemen; and at the adult end by the prolongation of
> the period of training for the increasing numbers in graduate
> school, a cadre caricatured by the psychoanalyst-in-training
> who at 40 is still his supervisor's "boy". . . .[2]

The passage merits elaboration. Examples of precocious
maturity are painfully common. The dean of students at a
university where I labored once described a telephone conversation with a somewhat anxious mother. It appeared that
her daughter was about to embark on a singing career, and
the mother wondered if the dean, a former jazz musician,
could suggest to her a nightclub where her daughter could
work without serious jeopardy to her reputation and her morals. The request seemed respectable enough and the dean
was inclined to be of assistance. Upon further inquiry, however, he discovered that the mother's concerns were warranted on grounds that he had not suspected. It turned out
that the daughter was twelve years of age. Whatever one may
think of a twelve-year-old girl belting out songs in a nightclub
during the wee hours, I would submit that that picture is at
least different from the sight of Becky Thatcher, dressed in
middy blouse and bow, timidly asking a reluctant Tom Sawyer to accompany her to a Saturday afternoon dancing class.

Pre-teenage entertainers are not common, but Little Lea-
guers in full athletic uniform vying with adult aggressive
competitiveness to vicariously satisfy frustrated adult yearn-
ings, are common. And the sight of children dressed in cap
and gown for an elementary school graduation is common.
There are countless more examples. Forced to assume an
adult role as a child, is it any wonder that the young have
some difficulty thinking like adolescents when they are

fifteen? The paradigm of such enforced maturity is simply, "too old too soon." A remark from a serious and dedicated Boy Scout leader summarizes it: "I find the twelve-year-old to be emotionally as developed as I am, and I therefore treat him as an adult." While there is no reason to doubt the accuracy of the man's observation, it may be true for reasons other than the emotional precocity of the twelve-year-old.

In his premature adulthood, the young person is reinforced by a number of significant factors, not the least of which is his role in an enormous and powerful consumer market. By choosing what clothes he will wear, and by determining what pop records he will hear, the fifteen-year-old is the controlling interest in a consumer market that reaches well over 16 billion dollars in sales per year.[3] If he wields the purchasing power of an adult, who indeed is to tell him that he is not an adult? The young can also feel a new solidarity with teenagers the world around. Tom Sawyer may have been a stranger to anyone outside of Hannibal, Missouri, but today's youth are kindred brothers and sisters to other youth in Boston, London, Rome or Tokyo who follow roughly the same styles, speak much of the same jargon, wrench their bodies to the same pop-rock music. Summer rock festivals have an international flavor the county fair never quite managed. Power is felt on an international level, and the young are very much aware of being bonded together in an adult world.

Extended Dependency

At the other end of the spectrum, as Riesman noted, the young person who has begun a kind of enforced adulthood at such an early age may be compelled by our technically sophisticated society to remain a child for far more years than he was ever asked to do before. Denny has referred to this as "extended dependency."[4] Precocity at the lower end of the developmental scale is matched with ever greater frequency by an extension at the upper end. Increased specialization and protracted professional training demand longer periods of study. Each year more college graduates continue their academic careers in postgraduate work. The term of academic study has been extended from college to the doctoral level in a period of about twenty-five years, stretching out the young person's dependency approximately four years. He once might have expected to be self-sufficient as a professional by the time he was twenty-one, but now he may be closer to thirty before he can make that claim. The same society that asked a precocious maturity of the twelve-year-old, now asks him to remain a school boy until he is well past twenty-five.

This conundrum produces the curious anomaly of a mature young man sent through college by his father and through graduate school by his wife. For over twelve years he is neither child nor adult, yet curiously a little of both. Indoctrinated into adulthood at an increasingly earlier age, he has been titillated by an early bait, but the bait continues to elude him in a torture that surely must rival the Chinese for maddening ingenuity. It is torture to try to preserve one's sense of integrity in a society that describes the mature adult male precisely according to his ability to provide. The ego of this gifted young male, supported by his wife, bringing home report cards from school when other males in the same apartment block return with their paychecks, is hard-pressed to preserve itself intact.

Extended dependency may be the price we must necessarily pay for an advanced technological society, and there is no reason to predict that it will pass in short order. But there is no intrinsic social necessity for early enforced maturity. The result is confusion. Lingering emotional traces and caprices of childhood mix with the adult precocity. Stages of development that have been skipped can be supplied in later life only with great difficulty. Usually the mixed childhood experience continues to haunt the adult in unconscious ways. It lurks beneath the consciousness of the young man who has always been told, "You're old enough now to tie your shoes, to run errands, to take care of your baby sister."

Turned thirteen, he looks at himself, decides that since he is as tall as his father, speaks with newfound strength, shaves on occasion, he truly is "old enough." At almost that instant, the melody changes and he is forthwith reminded, "You're not old enough to take the car, to stay out after midnight, to choose your own courses in school." This double standard appears to him as a cruel inequity.

Formerly, the transition from childhood to adulthood was made simply and cleanly by the magical device of some socially determined puberty rite by which the young person was whisked ritualistically from the world of the child into the world of the adult in a matter of moments. Today, there are no such rites of passage, and the transition, far from requiring but a moment of an initiating ceremony, may take as long as fifteen years. With the demise of the puberty rites, the previously described symptoms of adolescence—sharp sexual changes, oscillating moods, socialization into one's peer group, heightened emotionality and romanticism, petulant rebellion against authority, masks of fantasy—also disappear. We understood too clearly from our textbooks that the adolescent had to pass through this phase in order to emerge into the stark light of adulthood. And when all systems were passed—infancy, childhood, puberty, adolescence—the novitiate was over, and the individual was ready for life in the raw. Many of these characteristics, to be sure, are still appropriate for the young person, but they no longer fit with the same precision. What is emerging is a new individual, an adult-child created by a society that was too impatient to allow him to remain a child and too technological to allow him to become an adult.

Characteristics of the Adult-child

In a society where structures are regularly vanishing and previously accepted boundaries are disappearing, the adult-child must feel anxiety, a free-floating fear in the face of growing uncertainty. The world in which he has to grow is clearly different from the world of Henry Aldrich. The adult-child has known only a society in which there was TV, jet planes and astronauts, hot and cold war, rock and roll. He does not remember the Japanese of World War II, Pearl Harbor, the Depression, Knute Rockne or picnics at the park. His total experiential world is different, and astonishingly so, given the advances of technology in the last 25 years. Boundaries in space, morals, economics and politics have eroded. The Upper Volta, once distant and mythical, is but a few hours away, and men have walked on the moon. Henry Aldrich may not have cared much for his structure and may have rebelled in a timid way by smoking a clandestine cigarette behind the school locker room, but he knew what and where that structure was. Tom Brown, in the English prep school, may not have cared much for his headmaster, but he knew precisely what the old man expected of him. In terms of their structure, these boys located their place and took their bearings and consequently much of their identity from that well-defined structure. But for today's young person there are no such boundaries or structures against which he can take his bearings. In this state he is no longer just an adolescent. He is an adolescent in an adolescent world.

Illustrative of the loss of structure close to the adolescent is the contemporary switching and ambivalence of parental roles. From a patriarchal society, in which there was no question of the source of authority, we have gradually altered course towards an increasingly matriarchal society. Domestic decisions of schooling, religion and social manners are left more often than not to mother. I have not dealt with many troubled students in college who did not have an absentee father and a possessive, dominating Mom.

In many other ways the young person is also faced with the "breakdown of the generations." The usual distinction between generations has been lost, either because a mother is in competition with her daughter, or a father with his son, or the son has been asked to assume the role of his father, or a daughter for her mother. The family has become a society of friends rather than a hierarchical community. In the schools a feigned democracy has supplanted the autocracy of the prep school. The student is led to believe that he actually has a measure of control over the policies of the institution while the administration is pulling the proper strings from the wings.

Without structure, the young person becomes ambivalent and he hates oppressive and limiting structure while he unconsciously demands and needs it. In his zeal to free himself from oppressive restrictions, the young adult is caught in an agonizing limbo between successful emancipation and need for personal commitment. Freed from the tyranny of an old autocracy, he is not only emancipated, but he is, in Fromm's analogy, also alienated, alone, cut adrift, asked to rely on himself when he is not the least bit sure of who he is.[5] From out of this emancipated alienation, he needs to rededicate himself in a new bondage, a willing bondage, voluntarily relinquishing his pseudo freedom in the act of loving another person.

Today's adult-child is caught between the freedom of neo-emancipation and the freedom of loving commitment. So the language of love is supreme. Love is precisely what he implicitly knows he must experience in order to liberate himself from his own freedom and alienation and his structurelessness. The anguished need to commit oneself to another in the experience of a love relationship, coupled with characteristic self-doubt, can reach frantic proportions. The need in turn is amplified by the frenetic need to experience everything *now*. There may be no tomorrow. There must be an end to civil hypocrisy, bureaucratic irrelevance, political dishonesty *now*. On the personal scale, there must be total self-fulfillment *now!*

Above all, the adult-child is painfully subjective. With no structure upon which to lean, he must find an anchor within himself, and he must look to himself for the standards and objectives of his behavior. In the language of self-discovery and self-acceptance, to be sure, there is a whining petulance at times. "Symptom-acceptance" can replace the true exploration of self in tedious and sometimes painful self-examination. "Instant self-awareness" through acid or pot, reds or whites, "uppers or downers," beckons the young person to a magically self-fulfilled world by simply ingesting some drug.

With the same urgency the young person pursues creativity. One must be free to think divergently, to dip into the wellsprings of one's own primitive resources and withdraw a new art form, a new literary style, a new cultural modality. We have imposed a mandate to be creative on the young, and as a result, there is scarcely the chance to accept one's own mediocrity at any time. One *must* be creative even at the risk of being piteously banal.

All of this, the anxiety, ambivalence, loss of structure, the urgency, the need to be creative, stress the new emphasis on the self rather than on the structure. The young person is caught up in the social transition from a structure-oriented society to a person-oriented society, and in his own behavior he manifests all the agony of that transition.

The Myth of the Schools

The second adult myth suggests that high schools and colleges are not significantly different from what they were when we were in them some years ago. There is not much that should be said of this misconception. It is simply not so. The knowledge explosion alone accounts for massive change. As a college professor recently out of graduate school, I quickly realized that it was no longer possible to pass on to undergraduates what I had so recently learned in graduate school. The progress of the social sciences is that rapid. Socially as well, the era of the fraternities and sororities, of college football and panty raids is past. The atmosphere is charged, challenging, hyperserious and frenetically self-conscious. The agonizing soul searching and "encountering" of the young reflects their urgent need to find themselves in a society which gives no structure. As a result, the young are likely to be far more religious, but in a noninstitutional sense. Few students, even on allegedly Catholic campuses, feel any need to attend formal religious ceremonies. The religious experience is no longer identified with traditional institutional ritual customs and legal prescriptions. The young are building their own ritual. And it is futile to present them with injunctions from that institutional tradition. They have long since abandoned them as irrelevant, hypocritical and mechanical, and they are searching, even if unsuccessfully, for a more personalized experience..

Keniston has summarized this by describing the youthful phenomenon as the search for meaning and the cult of experience.[7] In 1966 Simmons and Winograd described the entire scene as accurately and graphically as any in their admirable little book *It's Happening.*[8] Anyone who attempts to reach the adolescent as counselor, pastoral or otherwise, on other than empirical grounds is sure to fail. It is in this respect a matter of knowing the territory. School counselors, educators and pastors have often been guilty of spending so much time examining their equipment and methods that they have neglected to note with any empirical care whether or not they were still on target. Heavy academic artillery is useless if it is off the mark.

Generations and Credibility

Not far from generation gap stretches credibility gap. Most of us, as well as the young, are lost in those wilds. We share a growing disenchantment with secular and religious institutions. The youth especially have observed that institutions, originally created to sustain some common experience, have grown larger than the experience itself and tend to suffocate rather than to sustain it.

Our political structure provided Americans with a dismal choice in the last election. While there was rioting in the streets, "politics as usual" was conducted on the convention floors where delegates persevered in cabalistic rituals that had little to do with representative democracy. That weird scene of a "due democratic process" indifferent to the cries outside seemed not unlike the assemblies and synods of the Roman curia where a traditional gnostic atmosphere prevails despite the gradual and relentless dissolution of religious communities and the total disenchantment of the young. The institutions are staring into the jaws of death, and are incapable of generating any other response but "business as usual."

The educational process, the young are told, must go on uninterrupted by dissent on the campuses, regardless of the fact that the "educational process, may mean simply the perpetuation of errors that have stolen into the academic world. "Maintaining the status quo" and "preserving the educational process" are rather meaningless shibboleths if the institutions are perceived to be essentially in error, sustaining a crippling double standard for the wealthy and the poor, the prestigious and the common, the white and the black. The youth want truthfulness with their truth. As Hans Kung has remarked, "the Church gave them truth, but as often as not did not give them truthfulness."[9]

As a young man, I often heard sermons in which the preacher began by apologizing after a fashion for his own inability to live up to what he was preaching with the limp admonition that ". . . upon the chair of Moses sat the Scribes and the Pharisees. Heed then what I say rather than what I do." This well-intended but tragically deceitful apologia will no longer do. Youth wants consistency between the "process" and the "content," between what is done and what is said. Pious reminders from Rome that ". . . our hearts are burdened by the sufferings of the poor in South America" fall on unheeding youthful ears in view of the fact that Rome does little to prevent her own South American hierarchy from perpetuating the violent and oppressive system that creates and maintains poverty and suffering for the masses.

In this dialogue words take on different meanings. "Respect for authority and law and order" gradually mean to the young a "tranquility of disorder" that tolerates injustice and impersonalism and reinforces an artificial society. Authority as the arm of an unjust power structure must simply be undermined, or else we conduct ourselves no better than the German war lords who were "simply carrying out orders." Youthful estrangement issues from general acknowledgment that the institutions and structures have become little more than games, collections of customs, rituals, regulations, habits, behavior patterns and judgmental postures that are now preserved for their own sake alone. Their options seem often too clear: join the system and play the game, fight it from within or drop out. The first alternative is a copout; the second is often futile, and the third very expensive. It requires great maturity, indeed the maturity of the Guru, as Alan Watts notes, to avoid these three obvious alternatives and challenge the system precisely by playing the game lightly.[10] The dissenter, be he a young political reformer or a dissenting religious, often fights against the institution he has abandoned with the same frenetic and hyperserious frenzy with which the dedicated and fearful defend it. If such be the case, it is clear that he has not quite left it behind. To do so requires much sophistication and maturity.

The Locus of Values

Through the yawning generation gap blow the winds of change, and any pastoral counselor who hopes to communiate with the young must know something of the anatomy of that change. When one sifts through all the varying characteristics that are the symptoms of transition, one factor emerges consistently. The gap is caused by a radical alteration of basic value systems, a change in the *locus* of values. Our American society has been historically achievement oriented. That is, of course, appropriate for a nation recently emerged from pioneer days and for a generation that suffered through the gigantic depression of 1929. For those who tasted the arid desolation of that depression, financial

security is not to be taken lightly. But an achievement oriented ethic is bound to be pragmatic and utilitarian. Virtues
are the means to an established end. Thrift, industry, responsibility and the credo of the Protestant ethic are the corner-
stones. A utilitarian value system accepts the basic structures
within which one lives as "given"; one has only the option of
selecting different means of working towards the goals set by
that structure. Success or failure in achieving those established goals is the measure of the good man.

But what if one challenges the basic structure? If one is
studious in order to be a success in school, to graduate high
in a class and matriculate to the "good" college, to study once
again in order to be admitted to the better medical school,
to study hard and then graduate to practice medicine successfully, what happens when the question becomes rather,
"What is the success of success?" What is the value of being
a doctor supporting by membership in the AMA an insensitive community?

The value system is no longer pragmatic; it is concerned
more about the ultimate questions. In this context, the entire
locus of values is different. Neither parties are making the
same basic assumptions about the "good life" and the nature
of the good society. The former accepts structures as they
exist and virtuously strives to achieve success within that
framework; the latter denies the structure and is committed
to its change. If the person is to become preeminent, above
institutions and societies, and if the structures are of value
only insofar as they serve the person and not vice versa, there
is little common ground in the value system. From the task-
oriented society of our past generation, we are moving to a
person-oriented society in which the value system and the
catalog of virtues is simply different. One is practically the
inverse of the other. Virtues once so prominent in American
life become the vices of a new society whose emphasis produces almost an inverse morality: put your dirty laundry out
and keep your best foot at home.

In the interest of this neo honesty, a young chap who was

suffering the ritualistic pangs of honest self-exploration in a college sensitivity group, begged a girl sitting across the circle to tell him exactly what she thought of him. Without guile, the girl answered directly and simply, "I like you." "No," the boy shouted. "I want you to tell me what you *really* think of me." Honesty had to be a negative statement.

In the inverse society of a new value system, the good old virtues become vices serving a sick society. The value gap is split open by the conflict of the person versus the structure, creativity versus conformity, individuality versus collectivity, honesty versus appeasement.

Bearing in mind the inverse society, the pastoral counselor must be aware that there is, after all, an exceptional similarity between the youthful dropouts of today and the early Christians. Both groups are paralegal; both are thought to be drugged or drunk by their more civil contemporaries; both practice strange underground rituals, and are questioned for them; both have informal but effective networks of communication; both are drawn closer together by common adversity; and both show a disdain for practical consequences. When warned to discontinue their underground and often subversive activities, the Christians felt they must continue. Warned that if they did so, they would be thrown to the lions, they persevered. There was nothing pragmatic or utilitarian about that value system. And when the neo dropouts are now warned and then threatened with jail sentences, they characteristically feel that they must continue their protest, must not allow themselves to be drafted for an unjust war, and are, for the most part, willing to endure the ensuing jail sentence. There is nothing utilitarian about that value system. Finally, both the early Christians and the neo dropouts were and are firmly convinced that they will overcome, that victory will inevitably be theirs, because for both the *locus* of values is ultimate, not utilitarian. Similarities prove nothing in themselves, certainly not identity. But similarities there surely are, and the pastoral counselor may not permit himself the luxury of ignoring them.

Notes

1. Edgar Friedenberg, *The Vanishing Adolescent* (New York: Dell Publishing Co., Inc., 1959).
2. David Riesman, "Introduction" to Friedenberg, *op. cit.,* p. 10.
3. *Ibid.*
4. *Ibid.*
5. Erich Fromm, *Escape From Freedom* (New York: Holt, Rinehart, Winston, Inc., 1941).
6. Kenneth Keniston, "Drug Use and Student Values," *op. cit.*
7. J. L. Simmons and Barry Winograd, *It's Happening* (Santa Barbara, Calif.; Marc-Laird Publications, 1966).
8. Hans Kung. Quoted from a public address given by Dr. Kung at U.C.L.A., November, 1967.
9. Alan Watts, *Psychotherapy, East and West* (New York: Ballantine Books, Inc., 1961), p. 64ff.

9. *Ethical Implications in Counseling Members of the Drug Cult*

It is at least inappropriate to begin a chapter by announcing one's confirmed conviction that the subject is not important. Nevertheless, many who have been working in or about the edges of the so-called "drug scene" are now quite convinced that it is essentially an unimportant phenomenon in itself. It is significant rather as a symptom of a larger, drug-oriented cultural malaise. There is, first of all, a dearth of hard empirical data relative to the effect of many of the drugs. Anecdotal material of varying quality prevails in an atmosphere of hysteria that surrounds the entire drug scene. This is not to say that drug usage, especially on campuses, is not widespread. But to focus on such drug usage as an isolated phenomenon is to concentrate on symptoms and lose sight of the essential issue: what is happening to our culture in general. With that caution, this chapter will devote itself simply to a consideration, however hypothetical, of some of the ethical implications involved in counseling members of the so-called drug cult, especially in the college situation, and attempt to relate those considerations to ethical norms on a broader sociological level.

The counselor on a college campus confronted with widespread drug usage is in the position of a tightrope walker balanced between the Scylla of the law and the Charybdis of the counselee. The situation is complicated by the range of postures that administrations on the college level have assumed vis-à-vis drug legislation and the implementation of that legislation on the campus.

Everyone is familiar with the fact that legislation on marijuana usage in the United States began with the Harrison Act of 1914. It was extended by the Uniform Drug Act in 1932 and the Marijuana Tax Act in 1937, which included marijuana in the legal family of narcotics.[1] As a result, possession, sale or possession for sale of marijuana in the United States is presently a felony, although sanctions have been diminished. This fact, of course, is known to all students, counselors and administrators alike. The situation with LSD is somewhat different because of the research devoted to the psychomimetic and therapeutic qualities of LSD since Hoffman's discovery of the synthetic drug in 1943. About 1961 the explosion in the use of the drug created a social problem of sufficient proportions that in many individual states specific legislation was passed. In California, in 1966, the Grunsky Bill was passed shortly before the state elections of that year. As a result of response to social pressures, we are now confronted with a crazy quilt of impulse legislation, most of it passed in an attempt to sweep the problem under a carpet. It is now a commonplace to observe that the laws are largely ineffectual, criminogenic, expensive to enforce, reinforcing to the black market, inhibiting to research to some degree and, paradoxically, incentives rather than deterrents to crime. The presence of such legislation brings the law in general into disrepute. Unfortunately, when there is greater hysteria, there is a tendency for more legislation to be passed. Whatever our feelings may be about the various laws, they are nonetheless still the laws. The university counselor then is often in the unique situation of acting in the face of legislation with which he would in large part disagree.

The second factor of note is that the drug cultist is by no means restricted to the college or high school student who makes regular use of pot, acid or speed and amphetamine derivatives. Indeed, our entire culture is in one way or another drug cultist. But for operational purposes, let us define the drug cultist here as an individual who "blows pot" frequently (for example on weekends), has "dropped" acid and other hallucinogenics on some occasion, manifests other symbols of the hip culture and is in danger of being "busted." We are confronted then with the specific situation in which this young person, defined roughly as an acid or pot head, is referred to a counselor. He, in turn, is being asked to determine the student's personal needs as opposed to supporting legislation with which both the counselor and student may disagree. In practical terms, the first function of the counselor is simply to notify the student, if he is not already aware of them, of the sanctions and risks involved in the continued use of hallucinogenic drugs. However absurd we may think the laws to be, the individual who dares to violate them must be prepared to take the consequences. In many instances, this will mean spending time in court or in jail.

Private Morality

There are four essential questions, I believe, vis-à-vis the ethics or morality of drug use. The first of these is the right of the legislator to invade the area of private morality. The bedroom and the internal forum are generally protected from intrusion by the public executive arm. In a recent decree, the Supreme Court, in a series of such decisions, defended the right of an individual to amass a library of pornography in the privacy of his own home. To punish an individual, therefore, for the possession of one of the hallucinogenic drugs seems to be in violation of this general principle. The law ought to restrict itself to actions performed in the public forum. Morality transcends the law, and is concerned, or ought to be concerned, with the private and individual sector.

Penal or Civil Laws

The second issue is the stance that an individual may take before a purely penal or civil law, in which there is no moral issue necessarily at stake.[2] Some laws do involve moral issues; others do not. Traffic laws generally speaking are in the area of purely penal laws. One would not normally consider it a moral offense to drive through a stop sign somewhere in the middle of the Mojave Desert. On the other hand, homicide, theft and antisocial activities are both penal and immoral. The question at this point, therefore, concerns the morality of the violation of a penal law when there is no question of immoral conduct. This is simply a matter of one's accepting the consequences of his violation. It seems to me fairly evident that unless one can successfully argue to the existence of some basic, personal, moral issues prohibiting the individual and private use of hallucinogenic drugs, the present legislation is penal only. The only moral issue involved would be the question of whether or not there should be legislation on that level at all. If we classify present legislation on hallucinogenic drugs as simply penal, at least with respect to possession of the drugs, morality is properly concerned with the matter of accepting the consequences for one's actions.

Personal Risk

A more intimately moral issue is the degree of personal risk involved in the use of hallucinogenic drugs, either to one's self or to others. The risk to one's self, in terms of brain damage, academic failure, etc., has not been empirically verified. That does not necessarily mean that there is none.

The argument that the hallucinogenic drugs lead to narcotic addiction, since virtually all narcotic addicts have at one time or another used pot or acid, seems to be too spurious even to consider. Even the scholastics would insist that *post hoc, ergo propter hoc* is anything but invincible proof. Despite alleged risk, one is faced with the many claims of mind expansion. Here, of course, we are confronted with an hysterically polarized society in which at one point the drugs are called the "dry rot of the human soul," and at the other extreme are thought to bring "instant mysticism." The truth clearly lies somewhere in between these two extremes.

Religious Experience with LSD

I should like to consider two points in this context: the nature of the religious experience which is allegedly involved in LSD ingestion, and the number or percentage of young people who are using LSD for this purpose, or are simply using the vocabulary of mysticism as a subterfuge and rationalization for otherwise motivated activity. The very fact that religious experience has been associated so often with LSD suggests that it would be rather naive to pass off this particular aspect of the psychedelic movement as a fad or phase and simply discount the claim of religious experience. For one reason, the use of toxic plant substances to induce some mystic feeling of communion with the gods and for meditation is not just a new fad. It has been known in primitive societies for millennia. Peyote has been used by the Indians in the southwestern United States for generations. A substance which they call *Teo-na-na-catyl,* or God's flesh, clearly represents for them a rite the eqivalent of a communion. In Mexico the crowning of Montezuma was accompanied by a mushroom rite, a religious ceremony. And in the area of the Rio Grande the use of peyote buttons or dried cactus plants has become the focal ritual of a religious sect identified since 1918 as the Native American Church.[3] The cry of the psychedelic religion consequently is scarcely a new one.

Ingredients of the Religious Experience

The primary dilemma in approaching this question is inherent in the very definition of what constitutes a "religious experience." This is a matter of our concept or notion of faith. But faith itself is a chameleon among human phenomena. It can mean many things. It can mean the assent to a series of propositions, or it can mean the more personalistic assent to a person, as in the case of one's belief in the person of Jesus Christ, Buddha or Mohammed. As an assent or response, faith is in some way observable. But as a purely subjective experience it is private and unobservable. St. Paul says that faith is the proof of realities we do not see.[4] This, I believe, is the sense in which we commonly use the word.

The dilemma arises when the believer states flatly that his faith has become empirically verified by some personal experience of what hitherto was not evident. It becomes a personal encounter with that which was previously unknown. The cloud of unknowing, a constant mystic phrase to describe the uncertainty which hung over the assent to the untested, has been lifted. There are many instances of the movement from the faith of unknowing to the faith of vision in Christian literature. Paul of Tarsus, for example, was picked up by God, thrown to the ground and blinded for three days; and in that direct experience, a religious experience, his faith somehow became known. The language of the mystics, used to describe their religious experience, contains a number of common elements.

Unity and Brotherhood

The first characteristic of the religious experience is the sense of oneness, of unity, of brotherhood, of a kind of cosmic togetherness. The empirical ego (which includes the patterns of our behavior, the ways one learns to cope with the environment, the defenses which one throws up against the environment) all are dropped in favor of an awareness of the inner world. The inner awareness generates what the mystics describe as the "all in one" feeling. One becomes identified with the inner self, the almost impenetrable core of self which for most of us remains shrouded in mystery throughout our lives.

Insight

A second operational characteristic of the religious experience is the quality of insight and omnipotence. There is in the experience a direct, intuitive, nonconceptual experience of the self which leads to an absolute certainty that the experience reveals what is profoundly real, and that all other previous empirical experiences are less real, even perhaps illusory. We reach beneath the games to find what is ultimately and primitively real, and that insight leads to a feeling of great power. Who could suggest to Paul of Tarsus after his violent encounter with the divine that he had not really met what was real, and that his profound personal experience needed further scientific certification? In the very experience itself there is the power that comes from the sense of ultimate reality.

Transcendence of Space and Time

A further quality of the religious experience is the transcendence of space and time. These dimensions become virtually meaningless for the duration of the experience. The subject of the experience tends to feel that of a sudden he stands outside time—in eternity or infinity—beyond both the past and the future. Time and space require some identification with the world around one, and with the loss of that identification the feelings of time and space are also lost.

Sense of Sacredness

Throughout both Christian and oriental mysticism, there is always a sense of sacredness, a silent, hesitant response to the presence of some inspiring value, as expressed in Rudolph Otto's term the *"mysterium tremendum."*[5] In specifically Christian writings one finds this in the literature of the sacraments. The original Greek for the word "sacrament" was *"mysterion,"* or "mystery," and it is precisely in the sacrament that the divine and the material are fused, and one encounters the two in one. This encounter with the divine through matter educes from the subject a sense of awe and reverence which is the prelude to worship.

Accompanying the sense of sacredness is a very positive feeling of joy, love, peace.The peace may be quiet or it may rise to an intense form resembling a kind of psychological climax. It is the "peace which surpasseth understanding," as much of the Christian literature has it. Anxiety is dispelled and there is a feeling of relaxation. In milder form it can be described as a kind of quiet tenderness.

Cognitive Change

In a rather different vein, the modes of thinking during the experience are said to be altered. Removal from the restrictions of the immediate physical environment make it possible for the mind to swing through empirically untestable realms. Contradictions, for example, which are rendered impossible in the physical world, are conceivable in a purely conceptual, dialectical world. In Hegel's idealistic world of thought, there is a coexistence of contradictory ideas. And so in the world of the inner self there is a kind of paralogic that violates all of the Aristotelian categories; and yet it seems at the moment, to the subject at least, to be eminently logical and sensible. One can claim to live and die at the same time; one can speak about being "in the body and out of the body" at the same time. In violent forms of psychopathology, something of the same process is described, especially by Arieti in his work on schizophrenia, as a paleological framework.[6] The individual can think he is both Richard Nixon and Jesus Christ at the same time, because these concepts, though somewhat unreconcilable in the empirical world, can coexist comfortably in the inner world.

Words and Experience

Finally, the religious experience can be described as one in which there is a conviction of the ineffability, the unspeakableness of the experience. Thomas Aquinas remarks that having attended the great banquet (a mystic experience) the Agape, or love feast, one finds himself incapable of telling anyone else about it. So intimate, so deep, so private it defies verbal description; there are no words for it; indeed, words kill it. All that one can say is, "Come and see." This characteristic can be exasperating to the listener who would like to have some description of the package before buying it.

Transiency

Generally speaking, the experience is transient, lasting perhaps a few hours or a few seconds. It can also lead to some discernible positive changes in the attitude of the mystic, of the religious toward himself, toward others, toward life and toward the experience itself. It seems to create greater sensitivity to others, increased tolerance and more real compassion in one's relationships with other persons. I am referring largely to the intrapersonal phenomenon Martin Buber describes as the "I-Thou" relationship in which the encounter takes place without the subtle and not so subtle masks that usually separate man from man.[7]

Especially fascinating is the fact that these characteristics are common not only in mystic writing but also in the psychotic condition and in the verbal reports of the drug-induced experience.[8] It is for this reason that Timothy Leary can say, for example, (and I believe with exceptional insight) that we do not rightly understand psychoticism because we do not understand mysticism. The psychotic, because the environment is altogether overwhelming for him, chooses to withdraw into the inner world where he is omnipotent, where he need not painfully check his thoughts against the world outside and where he is safe. For him, however, the experience may not be transient, as it is for the mystic, and the "self" which he reaches may be fearful and frightened. But the change in logical thinking, the loss of reality testing, the feeling of being momentarily at sea, are all part of the psychotic episode as they seem to be part of the religious mystical experience.

And, lastly, to the degree that one can accept the verbal reports of the psychedelic community, there is also something of the same ego loss which accounts for the mind-expanding qualities of which we read so much. Thus, in order to produce the religious experience, one must "blow one's mind."

Set and Setting

As so many authors have noted, any drug-induced experience is a function of the set and setting in which the drug is taken. The first is a semipermanent life style, and the second is the more changeable motivational element depending upon physical surroundings. What we are concerned with here is the life style, the predisposition for a religious experience. Even if a religious experience as here defined can be drug-facilitated, not everyone is disposed to have one.

The resemblance between the religious experience, the psychotic process and the psychedelic experience poses what I conceive to be an enormously provocative research question. What are the similarities and dissimilarities in the ego loss experience as reported by mystics, psychotics and acid heads? Some similarities we have already noted. The dissimilarities would appear to rest upon the person's readiness for religious experience, whatever that may be. We know precious little of this. It turns about the much larger question about the diagnostic differential between mystical experiences on the one hand and similar forms of psychopathology on the other. For example, is the asceticism of the Hindu fakir or the yen for martyrdom of the early Christian ascetic a form of violent self-punitive masochism, or does it really constitute the heights of a religious experience?

Research into the relationships between the ego loss experience of the mystic, the psychotic and the acid head could contribute considerably to the fascinating problem which lies in the netherworld between religion and psychiatry.

Risk vs. Gain

The question of risk must be weighed against the perceived gain. That there is a risk before the law and perhaps in psychological and physiological development is certainly true. But there is scarcely ever any growth without some risk. The responsibility of the counselor in this issue is to bring the student to the point where he can make a choice without coercion or custody and without need for social approval. He must be free to decide whether the risk is warranted by accurately perceived gain.

The critical and final ethical implication seems to turn about that latter point, the pursuit of a perceived gain. We are confronted by the possibility of some mind expansion. The moral issue here seems to be simply this: is it morally acceptable to attain synthetically what is better attained by arduous, anguished, personal effort? This is not a question of a legalized morality. It is on the basis of a morality drawn from the personal responsibility of an individual to develop his resources as seriously and as responsibly as he can, i.e., to actualize his potentialities. The essential ethical question, therefore, is not the legal one; but rather the regression to oral passivity to gain self-development by popping a pill. As has been noted before, this is an ethical implication not by any means restricted simply to the use of so-called hallucinogenic drugs or even the amphetamines. One could raise the same question about a drug-loaded culture in general, and the tendency to anesthetize one's self from the experience of even the most minimal pain by popping a pill. Such oral passivity is essentially regressive in a manner that is not in the interests of creative activity, and in a very personal context it must be considered rather immoral.

What we are raising here then is a new kind of moral question. Morality has through the agency of our Western tradition been identified mostly with laws. There must be, therefore, other grounds for determining personal morality. In this instance such grounds are found in the individual's unwillingness to face the painful aspects of self-awareness and development and to pursue these goals in an orally passive manner rather than in a personally active response.

In the consideration of the drug cult, there are two specific issues. One is the question of the validity of present legislation, one's posture in the face of it and the degree to which one is willing to assume responsibility for and the consequences of his illegal actions. The more profound question seems to be the norm or ideal which one is pursuing, the perceived gain and the manner in which the individual is pursuing the gain. This is the question that I feel a counselor, whose interest after all is rather directed more to the person than to the maintenance of a particular piece of legislation, ought to consider.

For the counselor, the essential issue is to lead the counselee to develop his potential by active rather than passive means. To do so, he must present himself as someone who is an illustration of such activity. What one is and does is more effective than what he says.

Unfortunately, morality in our Western tradition has been identified with law since the time that the Roman rite was imposed upon the Western Church. Along with Roman liturgy and Roman ritual came a Latin tradition which was basically legal. Moral issues became essentially considerations of the degree of violation of a law. The difficulty in this mode of legalized moral thinking is the fact that when one considers the law as the norm for human behavior, there is a tendency to think in terms of deviation from the law. Personal morality then comes to mean largely the degree to which one can depart from the law and still be safe, or the degree to which one departs from the law and must be publicly considered either a criminal or a sinner, depending upon the nature of the law. Casuistic thinking dominated Western morality. But if one makes the distinction between simply penal and moral laws, it seems unjust to think of morality in terms of penality or legality. In the more personal context, it seems more important to consider the norm in terms of an ideal which one approaches rather than one from which one deviates. The personal challenge, therefore, is not, "how far can I depart from the norm," but rather, "how close I can come to it."

Notes

1. 21 U.S.C., 171-188, 501, 4741, *et seq.*, and 26 U.S.C. 4701, *et seq. Cf.*, also Helen Nowlis, *Drugs on the College Campus* (Detroit, Michigan: NASPA Drug Education Project, 1967), pp. 31-44; William McGlothlin, "Toward a Rational View of Hallucinogenic Drugs," paper delivered at Student Personnel Administrators' Drug Education Conference, Washington, D.C. (Nov., 1966); Donald E. Miller, "Narcotic Drug and Marijuana Controls," *op. cit.*; Sidney Cohen, *The Beyond Within: The LSD Story* (New York: Atheneum Publishers, 1964); F. Barron, et al, "The Hallucinogenic Drugs," *Scientific American*, 210 (4) (1964), pp. 29-37.
2. *Cf.* Heribert Jone and Urban Adelman, *Moral Theology* (Westminster: Newman Press, 1956), chap. 3, p. 24, and other texts in moral theology.
3. William H. McGlothlin, *Hallucinogenic Drugs: A Perspective with Special Reference to Peyote and Cannabis* (Santa Monica, Calif.: Rand Corp., July, 1964), p. 9ff.
4. Heb. 11:1-2.
5. Rudolph Otto, *The Idea of the Holy* (New York: Oxford University Press, Inc., 1958).
6. Silvano Arieti, "Schizophrenia," in *American Handbook of Psychiatry, op. cit.*

7. Martin Buber, *I and Thou* (New York: Charles Scribners Sons, 1958); *cf.*, Buber, *Between Man and Man* (New York: The Macmillan Co., 1967, chap. 1.

8. Walter Pahnke, *Drugs and Mysticism,* unpublished doctoral thesis (Harvard University, 1962).